Casemate

FIGHTER ACES

------------------------------------>

Knights of the Sky

John Sadler & Rosie Serdiville

CASEMATE

Oxford & Philadelphia

Published in Great Britain and
the United States of America in 2017 by
CASEMATE PUBLISHERS
The Old Music Hall, 106–108 Cowley Road, Oxford OX4 1JE, UK
1950 Lawrence Road, Havertown, PA 19083, USA

Paperback Edition: ISBN 978-1-61200-482-2
Digital Edition: ISBN 978-1-61200-483-9

Printed in the Czech Republic by FINIDR, s.r.o.

For a complete list of Casemate titles, please contact:

CASEMATE PUBLISHERS (UK)
Telephone (01865) 241249
Email: casemate-uk@casematepublishers.co.uk
www.casematepublishers.co.uk

CASEMATE PUBLISHERS (US)
Telephone (610) 853-9131
Fax (610) 853-9146
Email: casemate@casematepublishers.com
www.casematepublishers.com

A lonely impulse of delight
Drove to this tumult in the clouds;
I balanced all, brought all to mind,
The years to come seemed waste of breath,
A waste of breath the years behind
In balance with this life, this death.

W. B. Yeats, *An Irish Airman foresees his Death*

This one is for the few: those men and women who saved us all.

CONTENTS

Prologue   7

Timeline   9

Aces of Aces   11

Introduction: Tumult in the Clouds   13

Chapter 1:   Above Flanders Fields (1914–16)   26

Chapter 2:   Bloody April (1917–18)   51

Chapter 3:   Their Finest Hour (1939–41)   81

Chapter 4:   War Without Pity (1941–45)   106

Chapter 5:   MiG Alley, Desert Skies and
             Stormy Seas (post-1945)   130

Postscript: The Last Aces?   154

Sources   157

PROLOGUE

MiG Alley; June 1953. In the contested skies over Korea, taking down MiGs was an obsession with American air aces; they were frequently very good at it. Major James Jabara was noted for his aggression, an 'excitable street fighter' as one friend put it. Lieutenant Dick Frailey, himself a veteran of 64 combat missions, was Jabara's wingman that day. Ironically, he was flying his commander's usual plane – the famous North American F-86 Sabre Jet, king of the south-east Asian skies, significantly outclassing its Soviet-built competition.

'You're shooting at me.' Such was Frailey's strangled cry over the radio as Jabara, from 3,000 feet, let off a burst from his .50 calibre machine guns, serious heavy metal, spent cases rattling from the wings to drop like sparkling brass confetti. He'd mistaken his own wingman for a foe. The fighter ace wasn't listening; he triggered another eight short bursts. These massive rounds tore into the wing, engine and canopy of Frailey's staggering plane.

His instrument panel disintegrated as bullets smacked between his arm and chest, any one of them potentially lethal. Smoke billowed from the engine, the aircraft stuttered, rolled then spiralled into a whooshing dive. Frailey fought the unresponsive controls, heaving the wounded plane round towards the blue expanse of the Yellow Sea. If he had to ditch, water was preferable.

'I don't want to eject,' he bellowed at the radio alive with calls from his comrades, 'I've got my new camera with me.' The camera was his pride and joy, an expensive state-of-the-art kit purchased whilst on leave in Japan. He wanted footage of MiGs in flight, better images than the grainy footage from gun-cameras. 'Screw the camera; I'll buy you a new one,' Jabara yelled back (probably the least he could offer). Eject Frailey finally did, but only as his fighter began its final glide into the ocean. His parachute opened correctly but folded over him like a shroud as he hit the water.

He had a job getting clear of the strangling harness only to find his one-man life raft also shot up and useless. North Korean guns lining the shore would soon be seeking him out as he floundered. Happily, deliverance – in the welcome form of a Grumman SA-16, an amphibious twin-engined plane used for search and rescue – came in under fire and scooped him up. Frailey lived to fight another day. The camera did not.

1853	First glider flight.
1898	Ferdinand Zeppelin constructs his first airship.
1903	First powered flight achieved by Wright Brothers.
1907	First British Army powered airship becomes operational.
1910	First ship-borne take-off and landing by an airplane.
1912	Royal Flying Corps (RFC) founded.
1914	World War I begins, first Zeppelin raids, first aircraft shot down by a machine gun.
1915	Gotha heavy bombers first equipped with synchronised machine gun system.
	L. C. Hawker receives the first Victoria Cross awarded for air combat.
1916	Mick Mannock joins the RFC.
	German ace Max Immelmann becomes the first aviator to receive the *Pour Le Mérite* (Blue Max).
	William Leefe Robinson, the first British pilot to shoot down a German airship over Britain, receives the Victoria Cross.
1917	First Sopwith Camel fighters come into service. German ace Manfred von Richthofen becomes commander of the Flying Circus (Jagdgeschwader I) and invites Ernst Udet to join him.
	British ace Albert Ball's Victoria Cross presented to his parents after he is killed in action.
1918	British Royal Air Force founded.
	Manfred von Richthofen killed in action.
1935	Invention of radar.
	First Messerschmitt Bf 109 prototype flight.
1936	First prototype Spitfire fighter developed.
1940	The Battle of Britain. Czech pilot Josef František shoots down 17 German planes.

1943   Polish ace Witold Urbanowicz (15 kills with the RAF in the Battle of Britain) goes on to down 11 Japanese aircraft while working with the USAAF in China.

Soviet ace Lydia Litvyak killed in action.

1945   The bombing of Dresden by British bombers.

USAF drop atomic bomb on the Japanese cities of Hiroshima and Nagasaki.

Soviet ace Ivan Kozhedub killed in action.

German ace Erich Hartmann reaches 350 aerial victories.

1950   Korean War begins, which sees the last use of propeller-driven fighters and beginning of the jet fighter age.

Soviet jet fighter MiG-15 'Fagot' enters service.

1964   American aircraft bomb North Vietnam.

1967   Soviet supersonic interceptor MiG-25 'Foxbat' enters service.

Arab-Israeli Six Day War begins with a pre-emptive air strike by Israeli Air Force.

1973   Israeli ace Giora Epstein downs 12 planes during the Yom Kippur War.

1980   Iran–Iraq War begins. Iranian ace Jalil Zandi achieves 11 kills during the war.

1982   Falklands War, includes longest bombing raid in history.

ACES OF ACES

Name	Country	War	Victories
Erich Hartmann HIGHEST-SCORING ACE	Germany	World War II	352
Ilmari Juutilainen	Finland	World War II	94
Hiroyoshi Nishizawa	Japan	World War I	80
Manfred von Richthofen	Germany	World War I	80
René Fonck	France	World War I	75
Billy Bishop	Canada	World War I	72
Ernst Udet	Germany	World War I	66
Ivan Kozhedub	Soviet Union	World War II	64
Edward Mannock	UK	World War I	61
Georges Guynemer	France	World War I	54
Albert Ball	UK	World War I	44
James E. 'Johnnie' Johnson	UK	World War II	44
Charles Nungesser	France	World War I	43
Richard Bong	USA	World War II	40
Francesco Baracca	Italy	World War I	34
Gregory Boyington	USA	World War II	28

Jean Navarre	France	World War I	27
Franco Lucchini	Italy	World War II	26
Sergei Kramarenko	Soviet Union	World War II; Korean War	25
Eric Lock	UK	World War II	22
George A. Davis	USA	Korean War	21
Witold Urbanowicz	Poland	World War II	19
Oswald Boelcke	Germany	World War I	18
Josef František	Czechoslovakia	World War II	18
Giora Epstein	Israel	Six Day War; Yom Kippur War	17
Lydia Litvyak HIGHEST-SCORING FEMALE ACE!	Soviet Union	World War II	16
Max Immelmann	Germany	World War I	15
James Jabara	United States	Korean War	15
Brian Carbury ACE IN A SINGLE DAY	New Zealand	World War II	14
Indra Lal Roy	India	World War I	12
Jalil Zandi	Iran	Iran–Iraq War	11
Mohommed 'Sky Falcon' Rayyan	Iraq	Iran–Iraq War	10
M. M. Alam	Pakistan	Indo-Pakistani War of 1965	9
Nguyen Van Coc	Democratic Republic of Vietnam	Vietnam War	9
Adolphe Pégoud FIRST AIR ACE	France	World War I	8

INTRODUCTION

TUMULT IN THE CLOUDS

> For a saving grace, we didn't see our dead,
> Who rarely bothered coming home to die
> But simply stayed away out there
> In the clean war, the war in the air.
>
> Seldom the ghosts come back bearing their tales
> Of hitting the earth, the incompressible sea,
> But stayed up there in the relative wind,
> Shades fading in the mind.
>
> H. Nemerov, *The War in the Air*

THE 1966 SCREEN VERSION OF JACK D. Hunter's *Blue Max* features George Peppard as the ambitious anti-hero, Bruno Stachel. The opening moments show him slogging through the mud of Flanders, squalor, death and despair around him. Mired in the very apogee of industrial warfare, he hears a Fokker Triplane in the perfect unspoilt sky above. He looks up and is entranced by this residual vestige of distant chivalry, some knightly paladin way above the filth, his machine painted a vibrant scarlet. No grubby *feldgrau* for him. Bruno knows where the glamour and glory is.

Reaching for the skies: The birth of the ace

That image has persisted. In the next war, while Tommy was lifted from the beaches of Dunkirk, exhausted, bloodied and unwashed, Hurricanes and Spitfires knocked down Dorniers, Heinkels and Me 109s. They kept knocking them down over the summer pastures of southern England and, in so doing, saved the day and possibly the world.

'The Few' became legend. Even now, if there is one military aircraft everyone knows, it's the Supermarine Spitfire. Its creator R. J. Mitchell died of cancer in 1937 – the development of the later versions which saw such splendid service was the work of his long-term collaborator and successor, Joseph Smith. Mitchell was dubbed 'the first of the few' in the 1942 biopic: a title which has stuck, leaving Smith sadly forgotten by popular history. Yet, in a way, the film represents something else: its inspiring myth of sacrifice and prescience endures because of the hope it held out at a time when it was needed most. Seventy-five years on and the Battle of Britain and the role played by the Spitfire is still remembered by many as Britain's finest hour.

It was a dream of glory, those aerial bouts. Fighting far above the choked morass, risking violent death in lethal jousts, it must have felt nearer to the tales of ancient warriors than to the world of Tommy Atkins. Each kill another step to fame. In reality it was very far from glorious; a hideous death from bullets, immolation or crashing just round every corner, with the certain knowledge that one day it would come. The survival rates were not encouraging.

Still, it was attractive. The silver aircraft soaring above a desolate hell of mangled trench-scapes endowed these flyers with God-like qualities; their exploits hungered after by a public raised on the chivalric tradition of Malory and Scott. The war on the ground could never be seen as any kind of crusade, 'the good fight' but, in the air, it might just be different. Even Prime Minister Lloyd George got excited:

The heavens are their battlefield; they are the cavalry of the clouds. High above the squalor and the mud, so high in the firmament that they are not visible from the earth, they fight out the eternal issue of right and wrong.

He went on to extol the divine qualities of the airman, not just as an individual warrior pitted against a worthy adversary but possessed of this truly Olympian power to dispense death from the skies. He shoots up enemy trenches and lumbering convoys, swooping like the hawk to devour his lumpen prey, 'every flight is a romance; every report is an epic. They are the knighthood of the war, without fear and without reproach.'

The post Great War literary output resonates with tunes of chivalry – *Knight of Germany* (the career of Oswald Boelcke), *The Red Knight of Germany* (von Richthofen), and *Guynemer: Knight of the Air*. Much of this self-reverential mythology ignored the reality of air combat. It was hard, exhausting, physically demanding, sapping morale and resilience, always dangerous. Yet the airmen, albeit frequently billeted under wet canvas, enjoyed better conditions than the infantry. The cavalry proper were largely redundant. Even when the war became mobile again in 1918, it was armoured cars and light tanks which led the charge. The long dominance of brilliant horsemen was at an end.

The idea of the ace, the celebrity warrior, persisted after 1918. But it was diminished. As the size of the vast aerial fleets expanded and the conflict, like some titanic Moloch (Lloyd George's words) saw ever larger armies thrown into the fire, the predominance of the ace declined. Britain and the other combatant nations had entered the struggle in 1914 with a relative handful of primitive aircraft. They were slow, flimsy, unreliable at best and not at all suited as gun platforms. The position a mere four years on was transformed. The big players all fielded thousands of fast fighters, reconnaissance planes, and the new four-engined bombers. Strategic air power had very much arrived.

Duelling in the heavens:
The evolution of the ace

The first recorded instance of aerial combat occurred in 1913, during the Mexican Civil War when American airmen Phil Rader and Dean Ivan Lamb, each hired by opposing factions, blazed away with revolvers from their primitive machines, a Wild West moment in the skies. Neither was hit. Once war was declared in August 1914, duelling above the fast-moving battlefield of that late summer became the latest fashion in aviation.

On 25 August, emerging French aces Roland Garros and Lieutenant de Bernis, flying a Morane Parasol, shot up a German plane which escaped by diving into cloud, though one of the two-man crew was injured. A few weeks later, on 7 September, a Russian pilot, Pyotr Nesterov, actually downed an Austrian Albatros. He did it by using his own plane, a Morane, as a weapon in a *kamikaze*-style ramming tactic. There were no survivors.

The first recorded actual victory was won by a pair of French aviators, Sergeant Joseph Frantz and his gunner Louis Quenault. They were flying a Voison biplane that, in their case, mounted a front-facing 8 mm Hotchkiss machine gun. This was possible because the engine was a pusher rather than a propeller, rear-mounted behind the cockpit, giving the gunner a clear field of fire. This was not a policy decision – Frantz had acted on his own initiative in fixing up the machine gun; his comrades in V 25 Escadrille ridiculed him for his 'Jules Verne' idea.

On 5 October, Frantz was on a routine patrol near the hamlet of Jonchery-sur-Vesle in the Rheims sector. He gave chase to a German two-man Aviatik and the enemy observer lifted a rifle, ready to open fire. Quenault opened up with the Hotchkiss. One round hit the German's fuel tank and the plane, belching smoke, smacked into a swamp. The pilot, Wilhelm Schlichting, was already dead, drilled by one of the Frenchmen's rounds, his observer Fritz von Zangen was killed on impact. First blood went to Frantz, who won the Légion d'Honneur and Quenault, who got the Médaille Militaire. The duel attracted a fair-sized crowd – 'all the French troops on the spot forgot the danger of passing shells and jumped out of the trenches to watch the air fight' (*Daily Telegraph*, reprinted in *Flight* magazine for 16 October 1914).

W. E. Johns served at Gallipoli as an infantryman but was commissioned into the Royal Flying Corps (RFC) in 1917. He didn't take to the skies over the Western Front until August 1918, piloting a De Havilland DH4 two-seater. He was shot down, and spent the rest of the war as a prisoner of war. His fictional creation Captain James Bigglesworth – 'Biggles' – did rather better, joining up aged only 17 in 1917. His fast, furious and successful career in the skies extended to nearly a hundred novels published between 1932 and 1999, the last some years after the author's death. Biggles embodies the romantic spirit of the ace, quintessentially English of course. Today he reads like the last hurrah of Empire before the word became toxic.

Biggles was a bit too dated for World War II. He was supplanted by Frederick E. Smith's classic *633 Squadron*, first a book and then a film. The hero Grenville, flying Mosquitoes, up there with Spitfires as one of *the* planes of the war, is more angst-ridden than Biggles, more taciturn and withdrawn. As the story opens, his crack squadron is to be sent on a near-suicidal mission to attack a German heavy water plant secure in some remote Norwegian fjord. But not before Grenville flies a solo

The **De Havilland DH4**, designed by De Havilland for Airco (hence 'DH') was the first British two-seater day bomber with effective defensive armament. Designed in 1916 it came into service the following year.

mission, one he hates, but necessary to eliminate any possibility of a captured agent being tortured into spilling the beans. The target is also his girlfriend's brother.

Despite the fury of the barrage, Grenville launches himself into the attack. Undeterred by heavy flak, the lone crusader pursues his unequal fight. When the Gestapo HQ comes into his sights, he gleefully strafes the fleeing torturers. The happy slaughter of these savage bullies is unmarred by concepts like 'war crime'. If the flyers are heroes so are their planes: the 'Mossie' would become an icon in itself. (The kit always counts as well of course. Planes are great fun, the realisation of man's long-held dream to reach the heavens.)

One of the finest memoirs to emerge from World War II and particularly the Battle of Britain was Richard Hilary's *The Last Enemy*. The author brilliantly evokes not just the spirit of the times but gets under his own and others' skins. He was a fighter pilot,who fought the Luftwaffe in those sunlit skies that summer, until he was shot down and badly injured. He was one of those who benefitted from the pioneering surgical treatments being carried out by Sir Archibald McIndoe (1900–60). The New Zealand-born plastic surgeon, famous for his 'Guinea Pig Club' of badly burnt flyers, achieved miracles in terms of facial and bodily reconstruction. McIndoe was building on the

The **Moran Parasol** was the 1914 Morane-Saulnier: a single-winged, one- or two-seater scout. The **Austrian Albatros** was the B1 which entered service in 1913. The **Voison-Farman Biplane** was an early model designed in 1907. The Aviatik B1 Biplane was a two-seater reconnaissance plane designed by Automobil & Aviatik AG.

techniques and experience garnered by his cousin, Sir Harold Gillies, pioneering plastic surgeon of World War I.

As a member of the 'Guinea Pig Club', Hilary underwent numerous operations on his badly burnt face and hands. He returned to flying duties and was killed in a second crash. He was 23. Before his death, he wrote: 'At this time the Germans were sending over comparatively few bombers. They were making a determined attempt to wipe out our entire Fighter Force, and from dawn till dusk the sky was filled with Messerschmitt 109's and 110's.'

He brilliantly evokes the drama and tension of the air battle, arguably the deciding round of the war. He also explains why he and his fellow flyers fought, something that had very little to do with chivalry:

> I would say that I was fighting to rid the world of fear – of the fear of fear is perhaps what I mean. If the Germans win this war, nobody except the little Hitlers will dare do anything. England will be run as if it were a concentration camp, or at best a factory. All courage will die out of the world – the courage to love, to create, to take risks whether physical, intellectual or moral. Men will hesitate to carry out the promptings of the heart or the brain, because, having acted, they will live in fear that their action may be discovered and themselves cruelly punished.

The Hurricane and Spitfire pilots of the Battle of Britain may not have been knights but they were heroes in every sense, all the more admirable for being so human, holding such ideals. Theirs was the good fight. For bomber pilots and crew, it was more ambiguous. They did not fight against equal adversaries in the air; they strove to avoid the fighters on their tails and their war was often waged against civilians. Arthur 'Bomber' Harris was unequivocal in his advocacy of strategic bombing, which including pounding the enemy's cities and their inhabitants into dust. Even at the time, the morality of hammering German urban targets was questioned. The bombing of Dresden in February 1945 is still regarded by some as an atrocity.

The fighter ace is seen as immune from such charges. He battles his peers and fights them in the skies way above the civilian sprawl below. He might attack ground targets but they're usually specific. He is the creation of industrialised warfare yet his pedigree goes back to the Greek heroes. He remains untainted by the serial horrors of war without pity. He is ideal for a war-weary public and propagandist media, hungry for morale boosters, for an individual to idolize. None who fought in the drab, stinking anonymity of the trenches became a 'megastar' like Baron von Richthofen or his fellow ace, Ernst Udet.

Fighter ace status survived the transition from piston-engined propeller-driven planes to jets. The Korean War (1950–53) witnessed the first air combat between the new generations of supersonic fighters. Korea was easily defined as a 'just war' – the United Nations was resisting North Korean aggression. However, American involvement in a later war – that in Vietnam – was rather less clear cut. The latter conflict became increasingly unpopular. Although viewed as an unequal struggle, the North Vietnamese air force was, by 1974, the world's sixth largest, though generally equipped with ageing or obsolete planes. This was little comfort to American pilots flying McDonnell Douglas F-4 Phantoms, Vought F-8 Crusaders and Republic F-105 Thunderchiefs as they ran the gauntlet of Russian surface-to-air missiles (SAMs) before even engaging enemy aircraft.

From the foundation of Israel in 1948, Arab-Israeli conflicts have witnessed much air-to-air combat, though the Israelis, normally ascendant, suffered from a devastating barrage of surface-to-air missiles during the early stages of the 1973 Yom Kippur War. These conflicts or series of conflicts have produced 50 aces, 47 of whom are Israeli. Colonel Giora 'Hawkeye' Epstein of the Israeli Air Force (IAF), brought down a total of 17 enemy aircraft to make him top gun.

The Iran–Iraq War (1980–88) was a bitter and bloody slogging match reminiscent of the Great War itself with huge loss of life on both sides. In the skies above the embattled deserts, scarred with incessant shell fire and the burnt-out carcasses of tanks, Iran produced at least two air aces. Brigadier General Jalil Zandi scored eight definite and three probable kills flying the redoubtable Grumman F-14 Tomcat, the highest score of any Tomcat pilot. Close behind came Brigadier Shahram Rostami, who claimed six definite kills; three MiGs and three Mirage F1s.

Modern asymmetric conflict, as in Afghanistan from 2001 and Iraq during 2003, doesn't involve air-to-air combat. Aircraft deliver air-to-ground strikes in support of conventional troops, Special Forces and allied militias, they don't fight each other for control of the skies. The pilot has good reason to fear anti-aircraft missiles but generally not the guns of an opponent. Increasingly, war in or from the air is waged by drones and computer-guided craft. The fighter-bombers of the future may dispense with the human, organic element altogether: it will become a war of robots, bloodless and impersonal.

There is an added, moral, dimension. Modern wars are fought out in the full glare of the world's omnipresent media. Recent tactical deployment of British aircraft in Iraq and Syria caused much angst in Parliament and there are ongoing (and wholly proper) concerns over civilian deaths.

Counting up

It's always difficult to assess claims of actual as opposed to possible 'kills'. The totting up matters because it's all too easy to believe more extravagant claims and come to a false conclusion as to the actual scale of enemy losses. Believing your own bull can be dangerous. In one daylight raid over Germany during World War II, American bomber crews collectively reported a huge cull of Axis fighters. Rather more, it turned out, than had ever been in the air... Many pairs of eyes had counted the same stricken plane so the tally had to be reduced by several hundred percent. The gun camera was introduced during World War II, partly in an attempt to promote greater accuracy. Yet even as recently as Korea both sides claimed a kill ratio of 10 to 1. Clearly somebody was unduly optimistic.

A number of factors fall into play. The incredibly fast-moving and ever-shifting three-dimensional nature of aerial warfare is not conducive to calm reportage. Pilots are stressed and frequently confused. There is also the desire to rack up your score, so a 'might have been' can easily become a 'probable' if not a 'definite'. High scores produce medals and these are naturally coveted.

Where combat takes place over one side's defined ground then it is easier – there will always be wreckage; enemy pilots will be killed or captured. For example, of von Richthofen's four-score wins, seventy-odd can be verified. The case with the Battle of Britain is less clear cut. Some 50 per cent of British claims do not tally with recorded German losses (though evidence from crash sites does support a number of these contested kills).

Achieving the coveted status of 'ace' is traditionally defined by kills. Generally, to qualify, a flyer has to have shot down at least five of the enemy. How quickly, indeed how easily, this can be achieved naturally varies. All-time top gun Erich Hartman flew over 1,400 sorties, fought air-to-air in 825 of those and shot down 352 of the enemy, an astonishing record. Hartman was a gifted combat pilot but many German aces scored highly during the halcyon opening days of *Barbarossa* in 1941 as the Soviets flung half-trained crews in obsolete planes out like chaff in the wind.

In terms of racking them up Hartman had some competition from the Finnish pilot Hans Wind who, in resisting the Russian spring offensive of 1944, *Bagration*, scored 30 kills in a dozen days. On each of three days he attained 'ace in a day' status! On 6 September 1965, during the Indo-Pakistan War, ace Muhammad Mahmood Alam brought down nine definite and two probable Indian aircraft. Next day, above Lahore, he bagged another five

Hawker Hunter Jets (a trans-sonic British fighter, which came into service in the 1950s). All in less than a minute!

The right stuff: What makes an ace?

What distinguishes an ace from lesser mortals? Is it just chance and circumstance or do aces have a set of shared characteristics? General Lasalle, one of Napoleon's dynamic cavalry commanders, the very epitome of a beau sabreur, once quipped that 'a hussar who isn't dead by thirty is a blackguard'. He himself lived only a few months past that age. The ace carries the same air of devil-may-care recklessness; he needs to be as skilful a pilot as the horseman is a rider. He has to look after his machine as he would a destrier. If the mechanics fail, he dies.

Prince Rupert, had he been alive in the 20th as opposed to the 17th century, would likely have been an ace, as probably would the Confederate lieutenant-general, Nathan Bedford Forrest. Hunting was always regarded as knightly training for war and the ace is, above all, a hunter. Erwin Bohme (an ace in his own right with 24 kills), who knew von Richthofen well, said this of him:

> Hunting is Richthofen's whole passion and for him the ultimate. And, primarily, he has to thank his hunter's eye for his incredible success. Watching like an eagle, he spots the weakness of his opponent and like a bird of prey he dives on the victim, which is inescapably in his clutches. As for flying himself, I believe he does not care very much for it…

An emerging body of work seeks to identify what makes an ace. A thesis by Katie M. Ragan of Florida State University, *The Warfighters of Today: Personality and Cognitive Characteristics of Rated Fighter Pilots in the United States Air Force* (2009), offers some illuminating insights. The author asserts that fighter pilots, putative aces, need a particular set of attributes that differ from those of the population at large, even those in other branches of the armed forces.

First among these is cognitive ability, the pilot needs above-average capacity for thought and reasoning, plus a fair measure of stamina. He's alone in the clouds, no buddy and no back-up. Training, instincts and reflexes are what keeps him alive. This is not about IQ – the study found fighter pilots did not score more highly than others who fly. But it did suggest that there was a greater concentration of high IQs amongst the combat flyers. The fighter pilot has to be able to multi-task, to manage speed, altitude, communications, weapons and all-round awareness at all times.

Emotional stability is another 'must have' – there is no room for hysterics in a cockpit. The wannabe ace needs to be able to focus objectively even in the red mist – emotional composure, stress resilience and confidence. Previous studies suggest that fighter pilots score heavily in key areas such as assertiveness, activity and in striving for achievement, less well in some of the 'softer' characteristics. A list of the ideal characteristics could be summarised as: aggressiveness, confidence, intelligence, assertiveness, self-discipline, loyalty, trustworthiness, decisiveness, diligence, endurance and dedication. If you've got all those then you've pretty much nailed it.

Motivation is vital. Any warrior needs to be motivated. It's not a continuum, even the most dedicated will waver. Exhaustion, cold, hunger all sap the spirit but to climb into that cockpit on a winter's morning, knowing you may face death, requires a very clear act of will. You can't just respond to orders or fall in with your mates. You're up there largely on your own; the sky is very big, lonely and dangerous, even without people trying to blast you out of it.

Are aces killers? Some probably are and might qualify as sociopaths, but most aren't. Their objective is to bring down the enemy. That some – like von Richthofen – exult in the hunt, the rush of the chase, is inevitable. Most Great War aces (though by no means all) were drawn from the ranks of those with the opportunity to develop hunting skills – typically gentry or upper urban bourgeoisie. It is a game bound to appeal to the hunter. The skills, patience and judgments needed are the same – the only real difference is that this game is firstly, never out of season and, secondly, shoots back.

Because I fly
I laugh more than other men
I look up and see more than they,
I know how the clouds feel,
What it's like to have the blue in my lap,
to look down on birds,
to feel freedom in a thing called the stick…
who but I can slice between God's billowed legs,
and feel then laugh and crash with His step
Who else has seen the unclimbed peaks?
The rainbow's secret?
The real reason birds sing?
Because I Fly,
I envy no man on earth.

Grover C. Norwood, *Skygod*

CHAPTER 1

ABOVE FLANDERS FIELDS

1914–16

> *The way the earth looked, falling; swallowing to stop deafness at altitude; the scream of wires; stars between wings; grass blown down when engines were run up; the smell – of dope, and castor oil and varnish in new cockpits; moonlight shining on struts; the gasps before the dive; machine guns.*

Cecil Lewis

MILITARY AND NAVAL AVIATION JUST HAPPENED. Nobody really planned it. Most generals thought airplanes were a temporary aberration. Even as late as the 1920s, Douglas Haig was extolling the virtues of the cavalry, untrammelled by the glaring reality that machine guns had dispensed with the art of mounted warfare forever and ever. As St Thomas Octave Murdoch Sopwith, CBE, of the Sopwith Aviation Company recalled:

> When we started the First World War, there were no fighters. The small, rather high-performance – for their day – aircraft that we were building were really built as scouts. From scouts they developed into fighters, literally – from going up with rifles and revolvers to the day when we learned to fire through the propeller. Development was so fast! We literally thought of and designed and flew the airplanes in a space of about six or eight weeks. Now it takes approximately the same number of years.

It was in the forgotten last gasps of the scramble for Africa that the airplane first saw service. The Italians deployed them against their Ottoman foes while relieving them of Tripoli in 1912. These were early Farman pushers, used for infantry reconnaissance. All sides in the tangle of the Balkan Wars of 1912–13 used aircraft. The very first automatic weapon to be mounted and fired from the air was a Lewis gun, fixed up on a Wright Flyer at Fort Myer Virginia. As early as September 1908 Lieutenant Thomas Selfridge had the unenviable distinction of being the first US Army officer to die in a crash; Orville Wright, who had been flying, was injured. There'd be plenty more.

The high command on all sides just didn't quite get it. The infant flyers were the new face of warfare. Gallant charges, drums and bugles belonged to romantics and movie-makers. This was the first great industrial war where competing technologies would ratchet up the scale, complexity and horror of conflict to levels of destruction never seen or even imagined before. Railways, wireless communications, fast-firing artillery, machine guns, bolt-action rifles, poison gas, flamethrowers, dreadnoughts, U-boats, tanks and above all aircraft were going to be game-changers. And there would be no going back.

1914: Clear blue skies

Take the cylinder out of my kidneys,
The connecting rod out of my brain, my brain,
From the small of my back take the camshaft
And assemble the engine again.

Royal Flying Corps Mess Song

After a brief and furious war of manoeuvre in the late summer and early autumn of 1914, the conflict swiftly bogged down into the mud-coated stalemate of the trenches. This network of labyrinthine scars slashing across northern France and Belgium, soon solidifying from Nieuport down to the Swiss border, extended over 400 miles.

And nobody was going anywhere soon; machine guns, trench mortars and barbed wire saw to that. Flesh and blood, all those squidgy organic bits, couldn't match the technology. Everybody tried and the young men of Europe poured out their bright lives' blood in torrents in the attempt. It didn't work.

In the air, the first faltering steps were being taken. Steps that would, in only four savage years, transform the scout plane into a fighter and immortalise many of the men who flew them, few of whom would last to write their memoirs. Even in 1914, the Germans, ahead of the game in so many ways, had developed techniques of aerial reconnaissance and observation. Scouting and reconnaissance was the old light cavalry role. But a solid trench line offers no flanks to work around and no scope for horsemen whatsoever. If you wanted to see what was over the horizon, you had to fly.

On the afternoon of 30 August, late summer heat lay heavily on the French capital, largely untroubled even by Count von Schlieffen's great idea, already unravelling on the ground. Leutnant Richard von Hiddessen, who had earned his wings three years earlier, flew overhead and, rather uncivilly, dumped

The **'tractor' engine** is where the propeller is mounted in front of the engine so the aircraft is pulled through the air whilst the **pusher** is one where the blades are fixed behind so the plane is pushed forwards. The advantage of the latter is that it is then possible to mount a machine gun at the front of the aircraft. The pusher type quickly became obsolete as aircraft engines grew steadily more powerful, by 1916 the pusher variant had had its day and the development of the interrupter gear removed its one advantage.

three bombs out of the cockpit onto the Quai de Valmy. Two people were killed and others wounded. These were the first unsuspecting and innocent victims of aerial bombing. From then on the 'six o'clock Taube' became a feature of Paris at war.

Britain had inaugurated the Royal Flying Corps (as part of the army establishment) on 13 April 1912. The corps (normally commanded by a lieutenant general and comprising a number of divisions) was a significant extension of the previous fledgling air battalion. It could boast both a military and naval wing plus a central flying school. Not to be outdone (and in the long-hallowed tradition of inter-service rivalry), Winston Churchill, running the Admiralty, set up the Royal Naval Air Service. In the equally important tradition of total parsimony, would-be flyers had first to qualify at their own expense through training at the Royal Aero Club.

High command was not entirely at ease with this new breed of airborne warrior. They rather smacked of maverick individualism, not something the staff would wish to encourage. Once war was declared, the RFC had to take on training its own pilots, most of who would transfer in from other units. Two questions were asked at the initial assessment; (1) why do you wish to transfer (not unreasonable) and (2) can you ride? They were already the new knights of the air. Most would train and those who survived would fly the Maurice Farman biplane, known as the 'Shorthorn' and powered by a heavy Renault engine. Being an instructor, even with dual controls, was at best hazardous, the attrition rate frightening.

For those first few summer months in 1914, in the clear blue skies above fast-moving battlefields where French *poilus* and mounted *chasseurs* wheeled, charged, and died, in uniforms Napoleon would have recognised, the flyers soared above, generally untroubled by their enemies. A kind of camaraderie existed, a gentlemanly enthusiasm for their art which made the idea of killing each other appear unsporting. That was not to last.

A 1913 recruitment poster for the Royal Flying Corps.

First blood

On 25 August, Lieutenant H. D. Harvey-Kelly, leading a flight of three from RFC No. 2 Squadron, gave chase to a lone Taube. Nobody had weapons so they harassed the German by what could be called tailgating, flying so close to his rear they were almost touching. Harvey-Kelly was a bare four feet behind, panicking his startled opponent who was also hemmed in by the other two RFC aircraft. The German pilot soon decided he'd had enough and ditched his machine on the nearest level field before bolting for the trees. He got away but the British pilots, landing behind, burnt his plane – first blood to the RFC.

Lieutenant W. R. Reid was one of those early RFC types who flew over the BEF's baptism of fire at Mons. His observer was called Jackson – in his diary Reid doesn't give his rank. Jackson was probably a captain as observers tended to outrank pilots; they were the senior partners in this aerial world. It was Jackson who, in halcyon summer skies above Charleroi, spotted a Taube (this could have meant any German machine at the time – the Allies had a tendency to call all German aircraft 'Taubes'). Reid had also seen the enemy but wasn't looking to pick a fight; Jackson was far more bullish:

> Jackson: 'Look, old boy!'
> Me: 'Yes, I know.'
> Jackson: 'I think we ought to go for him, old boy.'
> Me: 'Better get home with your report.'
> Jackson: 'I think we ought to go for him, old boy.'
> Me: 'All right.'
>
> I changed course for him and, as we passed the Taube, Jackson got in two shots with the rifle. We turned and passed each other again with no obvious result. This happened three or four times. Then, 'Have you got a revolver, old boy? My ammunition's all gone.' I, feeling rather sick of the proceedings, said 'Yes, but no ammo.' 'Give it to me, old boy, and this time fly past him as close as you can.' I carried out instructions and, to my amazement, as soon as we got opposite the Taube, Jackson, with my Army issue revolver grasped by the barrel, threw it at the Taube's propeller. Of course it missed and then, honour satisfied, we turned for home.

Despite those tentative steps taken with the formation of both the RFC and RNAS, Britain was the poor relation compared to her ally, France and even more so compared to the Germans. In 1914, the Kaiser sent his legions to war supported by 246 planes and seven Zeppelins, a combined ration strength of 525 flyers. In those early days, the eponymous Taube made up only around half the fleet. The rest were mainly Aviatiks, LVG and Albatros, collectively formed into 41 *Fliegerabteilungen* (which roughly translates as 'air divisions').

The French could count 160 aircraft and 15 airships serving with their Aviation Militaire. Their planes were a mix of Bleriots, Voisins, Morane-Saulniers, Farmans and Deperdussins. In many ways the French had led the field before August 1914. They had built many different models, tricky for them in terms of servicing but a blessing for their British allies who had virtually none. Obviously, they expected payment – entente only stretched so far. French and Germans differed in their engine preferences. The French used the rotary-model Gnomes and Le Rhônes whilst the Germans opted for the water-cooled inline power unit.

That summer the RFC went to war with a mere handful of squadrons, each of them capable of fielding three flights each of four machines. In all, they could muster no more than 113 planes and six airships. Of the available aircraft only 63 actually went over to France with the British Expeditionary Force (BEF). Very quickly, even this modest resource proved

Count Ferdinand von Zeppelin (1838–1917) was the designer of a type of rigid airship, all which would be branded after him. He was designing zeppelins as far back as 1874 but it wasn't until 1910 that Deutsche Luftschiffahrts-AG commenced the first commercial flights. During World War I zeppelins were used extensively both for reconnaissance and bombing. Over 500 Britons would die in Zeppelin and bomber raids.

its worth. It was French aviators who spotted the crucial gap opening up between the German armies seeking to manoeuvre around Paris. This was the final unravelling of the Schlieffen Plan and the cue for Joffre's timely riposte on the Marne. Even earlier the RFC had detected the German outflanking movement at Mons that could have led to the encirclement of the diminutive BEF and a catastrophic defeat.

More firepower

The difficulty with actually fighting in the air was the installation of the machine gun. Pistols and rifles, used Wild West style, were all very box office but ineffective in combat. Some pilots even took to securing grenades below the fuselage as a kind of exploding flail with which to scourge the opposition. This might have been biblical but it wasn't very practical. There was no point in having a machine gun fitted above the engine cowl if the first thing it would do was to blast off the propeller. This was a total handicap for tractor-powered planes but mounting machine guns also caused problems for pushers. Here, the weight of the gun would interrupt the fragile aerodynamics of the machine and slow it down, so the unarmed prey could quickly sprint to safety before the hopeful predator was able to close in for the kill.

Lieutenant Louis Strange, flying with No. 6 Squadron, had experimented with mounting a machine gun onto his Farman. This kite was replaced by a Martinsyde Scout, which his commanding officer handed over after much cajoling (there was always earnest jostling when new planes arrived). His new machine proved something of a turkey. It was slow, unstable and unresponsive, not quite the ace's ideal. It did have a forward-firing Lewis mounted on the top wing. This could be fired from the cockpit but the drum magazine, once expended, had to be changed by hand – while the pilot was also trying to fly the aircraft.

Undeterred, Strange, hungry for spoils, set off on a solo patrol deep into enemy airspace. He spotted an equally lonely Aviatik flying above and in a northerly direction. His lumbering plane struggled to catch up as the drag of the wing-mounted Lewis slowed the Martinsyde down to a sedate 60 mph. Strange was soon seen and the German pilot made a run for it. Both were pretty much maxed out in terms of height so, from a distance, he chanced a burst. This neatly emptied the magazine without appearing to inconvenience the enemy.

Now to change the magazine. He tried to use one hand to free the empty drum as he turned for home. As he was dropping altitude his speed had rocketed to 75 mph, pretty much flat out with quarter of an hour's flying time back to Allied lines. The wind howled in his face and his gloved fingers, already stiff with cold, couldn't get a decent grip on the drum which was now seemingly jammed. There was nothing for it but to stand up in the cockpit, strip off his gloves and attempt, using both hands, to wrench the magazine free. This meant twisting the drum against its spring load. He had the joy stick between his knees, attempting by acrobatics to keep his beast of a plane on a level course.

As he heaved on the drum, the Martinsyde lived up to its bad press: the port wing slanted sharply. He unwittingly shifted against the control which now sent the plane into a full roll. He was chucked out of the cockpit and found himself a mere second or so later hanging onto the drum for dear life as the plane flew on upside down. The jammed magazine, still happily stuck, was all that was preventing him from a fall of 9,000 feet. This was not a happy situation. He was aware that only a crossed thread was keeping him airborne.

He was about to test just how jammed this particular jam was as, aping a circus performer, he used it for leverage to haul himself up to his elbows, attempting to hook a leg over the inverted upper wing. Astonishingly, at the third attempt, he succeeded. He wasn't out of the woods yet, very far from it. The plane, as its speed fell, went into a dive. This was dangerous when you were at the controls; clinging to one wing, it was really most unwelcome. G forces and his churning insides were both trying very hard to hurl him off the wing. The plane had lost 2,000 feet of height. Somehow, with almost superhuman strength and nerves of tungsten, he clawed his way back into the pilot's seat. He was now only 1,500 feet above the trenches.

He finally succeeded in getting control, wresting the aircraft out of its death spin and getting back to his aerodrome otherwise unscathed. His commanding officer could have been impressed but wasn't. Strange was censored for causing 'unnecessary damage' to both instruments and the seat through his frantic acrobatics. It wasn't just the infantry who relied on bull.

1915 – The Fokker Scourge

If by some delightful chance,
When you're flying out in France,
Some old Boche machine you meet,
Very slow and obsolete,
Don't turn round to watch your tail,
Tricks like that are getting stale;
Just put down your bally nose,
And murmur, 'Chaps, here goes!'

To the tune of: *Tonight's the Night*

1915: the year of stalemate, when the war of manoeuvre seemed as distant as Mars; there were in total some 25,000 miles of trenches snaking along the Western Front. France and Britain tried to break the deadlock, they failed. Offensives in Artois resulted in tens of thousands of casualties, many of whose bones still crowd the ossuary at Notre Dame de Lorette. The front line of trenches barely moved, mired in blood and unimaginable squalor. Above, the skies were getting much busier. Conflict is a great spur to innovation and the transformation of aerial warfare was already underway.

It was the British who introduced the first purpose-built 'fighter'. This was the FB5. But this wasn't the plane that would come to symbolise the fighting in the air from the summer of 1915 onwards. As the armies stalled in mud and wire, the Germans produced Fokker's EI, an *Eindecker* or monoplane with a single forward-firing Parabellum machine gun. The key innovation was the synchronisation gear, which enabled the pilot to fire through the propeller.

Roland Garros, an experienced flyer even at the outbreak of war, had worked with plane manufacturer Raymond Saulnier. He fitted deflector plates to the propeller and mounted a machine gun. After his first kill, Garros downed four more during early April 1915. His run ended on the 18th when a lucky rifle shot (he might have differed about the use of the word 'lucky') disabled the motor, forcing him to crash land behind enemy lines. He tried to set fire to the plane but was captured, along with his precious deflector plates. Garros escaped from captivity in 1918 and flew again. He was killed in action barely a month before the armistice.

Cue Anthony Fokker, the brilliant Dutch aeronautical engineer and designer. He examined Garros' deflector plates and decided

The argument over whether **air-cooled radial** or **liquid-cooled inline engines** were superior raged throughout World War I. Radials were lighter: weight was always critical and the radials could take more punishment in the fight. They were, in the early days at least both simpler and more reliable. What they lacked was power and the design impeded the pilot's visibility, critical in dog-fighting.

he could do better. When he arranged a factory demonstration of the new interrupter gear, those German staff officers present remained unconvinced it would work in combat. They wanted the real thing not a simulation and they insisted Fokker undertake the test mission himself. This might have been a salesman's nightmare but he went up anyway, seeking out some unsuspecting Frenchman for target practice.

He was flying at around 6,000 feet when he spotted a sedate Farman two-seater, cruising a couple of thousand feet below. This was a pusher plane which didn't detect the hawkish Eindecker as Fokker swooped down. The French pilot appeared not to have seen him – he was now a sitting duck. When the crew did realise they were under attack, they appeared to remain unconcerned. After all planes didn't carry machine guns so the risk was pretty small. Fokker was aware the Frenchman was his for the taking, pulling the trigger would send a storm of lead into fabric and flesh.

Fokker was on the brink of making his point emphatically when he hesitated. After all, he had nothing personal against these individual French flyers; he was only seeking to prove that his design would work. Building weapons isn't the same as using them and he didn't open fire. His imagination could picture his bullets rupturing the fuel tank and incinerating the crew. He decided he had made his point and no bloodshed was needed. Curtly, he informed his would-be buyers they would have to accomplish that bit for themselves. They soon did.

The Eindecker was to herald the time of 'the Fokker Scourge' – the new plane gave Germany a burst of hegemony. This wasn't because it was all that good, but it was better than anything the British or the French could put up at that stage. In 1915, the Fokkers were doled out to protect vulnerable two-seaters rather than being formed into fighter squadrons. If that had been achieved, the Allies would have fared far worse. Essentially, the German mentality was defensive. Overall, the Allies had built up a numerical superiority that was harnessed to aggressive tactics, constantly flying offensive patrols over enemy lines. Even by the end of 1915, there were only a hundred or so fighters available to the Germans on the Western Front even though the Eindecker had spurred several competitors, the Pfalz and Halberstadt DII.

The first aces

Bavaria, though part of the Kaiser's *Reich*, had a strong tradition of independence. It was the South German wing of the air service which formed the first three bespoke (if ad hoc) fighter groups, latterly the brilliantly named *Kampfeinsitzer-kommando* or KEK, combat single-seater commands. This facilitated the rise of two men who were to symbolise the emerging cult of fighter aces – Max Immelmann and Oswald Boelcke. In January 1916 both would be awarded the *Pour le Mérite* – the legendary 'Blue Max'; Germany's highest gallantry award. For an ace, it was the badge of stardom. Celebrity was becoming important. Propagandists on both sides realised that these heroic lone wolves offered the cloak of chivalric glamour in this most un-chivalrous of wars. It was on that day perhaps that the fighter ace fully 'arrived'.

Immelmann, 'the Eagle of Lille', was famed not just as a fighter ace but as a technical innovator of the half-loop, half-roll combat tactic, 'the Immelmann turn'. Born in 1890, he was an early enthusiast for flying. He was sent for pilot training in November 1914. He was a gifted student but, like von Richthofen, something of a loner, devoted to his mother and his dog and not imbued with the boisterous camaraderie of the mess. His early missions were entirely reconnaissance. In June 1915 he was shot down by a French Farman, only to emerge unscathed and with an Iron Cross (second class).

The arrival of the Eindecker at Douai aerodrome was the spark that ignited both his and Boelcke's careers. On 1 August ten

British planes shot up and bombed the airfield. Both German aviators leapt for their machines and mounted hot pursuit. Boelcke's gun jammed, forcing him out of the fight. Immelmann did rather better. He took on two of the Brits and forced one down. Though wounded the Englishman landed safely and Immelmann courteously took him prisoner. This exploit earned him another Iron Cross, this time first class.

In the third week of September he brought down two more victims but was himself shot down a couple of days later when a French Farman peppered his fuel tank and shot away his wheels. He walked away from the wreck and, undeterred, chalked up kill no 4, another British plane, above Lille. He downed another over Arras and the sixth on 7 November. Just over a month later on 5 December he claimed a French Morane. By the standards of 1915, seven kills was a lot. The war in the air hadn't reached the immense numbers of 1917–18. He and Boelcke became rivals that autumn, matching score for score.

One Royal Aircraft Factory BE2c was luckier. Captain O'Hara Wood was flying with Ira Jones as observer. The single Lewis gun operated by Jones had a series of mounts and for a full traverse had to be swapped between these. No easy matter especially when, as they'd dreaded, a lone Eindecker began stalking them over Lille. The hunter manoeuvred below and behind, the classic blind spot and came in gun blazing. Jones, unable to swap the Lewis fast enough, grabbed it and tried to fire holding the cumbersome weapon with its fearsome recoil like a Tommy gun. Not a great idea. The gun, like a living thing, leapt free of his hands and disappeared overboard. They were defenceless but Immelmann had run out of ammunition and flew off. Wood and Jones lived to fight another day.

It was on 12 January 1916 that the two rival aces both downed their eighth opponent. Eight kills was enough to win a coveted Blue Max, the talisman of success. With other manufacturers hot on his heels, Fokker attempted to up-gun the EIII model by adding two more machine guns and beefing up engine

The Pour le Mérite, or the 'Blue Max', Prussia's highest military order, seen here worn by Manfred von Richthofen in around 1917.

performance. In April 1916, Immelmann tested the new plane but the interrupter gear just couldn't handle three guns and he shot himself down. Even two proved tricky and led to another crash in May.

Nonetheless, by early June he'd scored 15 victories. On the 18th his considerable luck ran out. He got into a dogfight with some of the 'pushers' of 25 Squadron. In the melée Lieutenant G. R. McCubbin and Corporal J. H. Waller claimed they'd hit Immelmann's Fokker, causing his fatal crash. German sources claimed it was anti-aircraft fire, 'Archie' as it was known, that brought him down. Fokker himself was prepared to accept this verdict as it neatly avoided any questions about the working of the interrupter gear. Immelmann's brother Franz was convinced otherwise, claiming he'd examined the wreckage and found the propeller shot in half. Whatever actually occurred, the first true fighter ace passed into legend.

Oswald Boelcke was far more gregarious. Born a year later in 1891; he was an outstanding young sportsman and enthusiastic advocate of aggressive German militarism. At 13, he wrote a personal letter to the Kaiser asking for a place at a military academy. His turn came in 1914 – at Darmstadt he had his first taste of flying. He was still only an NCO for, in those very early days, the observers had most of the kudos, flyers were just the ones who drove. His older brother Wilhelm had also joined up and both won gallantry awards during that first year.

Boelcke was grounded by illness for a period but, early in 1915 he was assigned to Aviation Section 62 where he met his rival Immelmann. By the start of 1916, he was a star and, in January scored another four kills. These included a Vickers FB5, another two-seater pusher. Although these were rapidly approaching obsolescence as a design, they were very agile in the air and this crew gave Boelcke quite a fight. The two duelled for over half an hour, the pusher's gymnastics enough to deny him a killing burst. The Englishman's luck ran out almost directly above Boelcke's own aerodrome at Douai.

He was not only a hit in Germany, he also won a decoration from the French. Nothing to do with flying this time, he had averted tragedy when a local lad slipped into the canal. Boelcke, a strong swimmer, dived in to rescue the boy from certain drowning. The French government awarded him a life-saving medal, though obviously not in person.

In February 1916, the great German offensive at Verdun opened up, the fearsome shrieking of the guns a doleful summons to months of hideous attrition. Boelcke's *jasta* (fighter squadron) flew into this sector. Their prime role would be reconnaissance but on 13 March he clashed with a lone Voisin and set off in pursuit. The much slower French plane, pilot already rattled, made for the sanctuary of the clouds. The next Boelcke saw of it, the hapless observer was engaged in a desperate bid to stabilize the unwieldy brute of an aircraft by clambering out onto the wing.

This wasn't recommended in any textbook or manual. Boelcke lacked the innate cruelty which spurred his successor von Richthofen and refrained from firing. It didn't really matter as a sudden lurch sent the Frenchman off into the clouds and the long, very lonely fall to his death. Within a few days Boelcke had added another three Farmans to his growing tally.

The battles of 1916, across the ravaged landscapes of pounded fields and skeletal forests, grew larger and more intense, dwarfing anything that had gone before. So too in the skies. By September

1916, Boelcke was leading Jasta 2, equipped with the much-feared Albatros DII. He had his pilots fly in big formations, 'circuses' as the Allies dubbed them. Flying these formidable, fast fighters Boelcke pushed his score up to 40. In September alone, now battling over the Somme, he downed 11 British planes. He was Germany's top ace yet he had none of the hubris that often went with that status. His belief was that victories belonged to the unit, more than the individual. It is perhaps ironic that one of his most promising novices was Manfred von Richthofen, the man who would come to exemplify the self-seeking glory of the individual hunter.

Boelcke was an inspirational and conscientious leader. He trained and mentored his pilots exhaustively and preached the gospel of successful air combat throughout the German air service. He issued his tactical doctrine for dog-fighting early in 1916 as the great battle for Verdun was beginning to unfold. This is the voice of experience:

(1) Always try to secure an advantageous position before attacking. Climb before and during approach in order to surprise the enemy from above, and dive on him swiftly from the rear when the moment to attack is at hand.

(2) Try to place yourself between the sun and the enemy. This puts the glare of the sun in the enemy's eyes and makes it difficult to see you and impossible for him to shoot with any accuracy.

(3) Do not fire the machine guns until the enemy is within range and you have him squarely within your sights.

(4) Attack when the enemy least expects it or when he is preoccupied with other duties such as observation, photography or bombing.

(5) Never turn your back and try to run away from an enemy fighter. If you are surprised by an attack on your tail, turn and face the enemy with your guns.

(6) Keep your eyes on the enemy and do not let him deceive you with tricks. If your opponent appears damaged, follow him down until he crashes to be sure he is not faking.

It was on 28 October that Boelcke's store of luck ran dry. All pilots, aces especially, lived with the knowledge that their life expectancy was finite. For beginners, it could be measured in weeks, sometimes days. With no parachutes the only hope was to nurse a stricken plane into a soft landing somewhere. Few slept well when they were set to fly the dawn patrol, that mystical time when light filters and brightens as the new day rises. Up at 04.30 with a brew of tea or cocoa and perhaps a shot to calm the nerves, then out and into the cockpit, the loneliest place on earth. This is five o'clock in the morning courage, no red mist or heat of battle, no comfort of comradely cloth at the touch. Each patrol may be your last, the way to flaming death. Pilots carried revolvers and pistols, not for cowboy antics but to spare themselves the agony of burning alive.

On that day, Boelcke had von Richthofen and Erwin Böhme as his wingmen, six Albatroses in the patrol. They dived to scrap with some DH2s and Böhme flew that bit too close, that second of inattention. His wing sliced clear through his chief's upper wing struts, like a knife through cheese. The wing collapsed; all torsion and strength gone and Boelcke plummeted to his death. Ironically, he did manage to crash land the crippled Albatros but he had forgotten to fasten his seat harness and was killed on impact.

Erwin Böhme, born in 1879 and, like his boss, a serious sportsman, was devastated by the accident for which he blamed himself. Indeed, at one point, he became suicidal. Von Richthofen (nobody's first choice for counselling perhaps) managed to talk him out of it and he went on to score 24 kills and win the Blue Max. He was killed in action on 29 November 1917.

Oswald Boelcke was buried in Cambrai Cathedral to a packed house, ablaze with gold braid. Even British prisoners of war from Osnabrück sent a card and the RFC dropped a wreath. There was still some romance left, for the moment anyway.

1916: The big push

Oh, we've come up from Fifty-four [Squadron]
We're the Sopwith Pups you know,
And wherever you beastly Huns may be
The Sopwith pups will go.
And if you want a proper scrap,
Don't chase Es any more,
Because we'll come up and do the job,
Because we're Fifty-four

Sung to the tune of: *We've come up from Somerset*

Haig, now commanding the BEF, and 'Papa' Joffre thought 1916 would be the year that a great Franco-British offensive would 'kick Jerry all the way back to Berlin'. Erich von Falkenhayn had other ideas; he was planning to knock France out of the war by immolating her army in a vast cauldron battle at Verdun. He very nearly succeeded. Joffre begged Haig to launch a summer offensive on the Somme. This proved to be the Calvary of Kitchener's volunteers, 57,000 on the first day alone. As the stakes rose on the ground, the war in the air just got bigger and bigger. By mid-November total British casualties on the ground would stand at 420,000.

For the pilots, observation and spotting remained paramount. Second Lieutenant Alan Bott was seconded from the gunners – in his case the Royal Garrison Artillery (RGA) – to 70 Squadron where he flew patrols as an observer over the vast charnel house of the Somme battlefield. He had some lively times in the autumn of 1916.

Like all destined to fly with the dawn, he was woken at 04.30 by his batman with a cup of strong cocoa. By 05.00, the crews were kitted up in their heavy flying coats, helmets, scarves, gloves and sheepskin-lined boots, Michelin men rather than the sleekly uniformed heroes of recruiting posters and movies. It was barely getting light and the roar of engines as their Sopwith 1½ strutters fired up shattered the pre-dawn stillness, 'giving dreadful note of preparation'.

Chocks away and their machines trundled forward, taxiing over the strip, a light bounce and then rising into morning air. By now the opaque grey of dawn was giving way to sunrise, streaks of red in a lightening sky. It's a good time to be alive, even if you're flying towards death. The rendezvous was at 3,000 feet as the patrol headed off north and east towards Bapoume, the final objective of Haig's big push and one that would elude every last gasp of the offensive. Below, a mosaic of dun-coloured fields with patches of bright green woodland, pastoral calm then, almost suddenly, the arid wasteland of the Front. A dense belt and maze of trenches slicing across the earth, a landscape unimaginably altered in a minute's flying time. Then no man's land, that cratered, eviscerated, nightmare of wrecked and bloated ground.

Once over enemy lines, everyone test-fired their guns, short rattling bursts, staccato above the steady hum of engines. Bott spotted eight enemy planes below, racked up in stepped formation like the rungs of a Venetian blind. They weren't alone; enemy fighters were circling above but Bott's pilot dived on the prey below. At least one German, probably a Roland biplane, had other ideas and fastened on their tail. The British pilot jinked and banked, the enemy overshot providing Bott, with the Lewis gun, a perfect target.

The **Sopwith 1½ strutter** was introduced in 1916 as a twin-seater fighter and reconnaissance aircraft. It was quick and agile, the best of the breed so far on either side. It came with a synchronised Vickers .303 for the pilot and a Lewis for the observer. In September its smaller single-seater brother the Pup took to the air equivalent to the nimble Nieuport 17 adopted by the French in March.

He got off three rounds before the beastly gun jammed – an all too frequent occurrence. He tried re-cocking, no result. One live round had racked up against a spent case which had failed to eject. He'd have to half strip the gun to clear the blockage. Meanwhile the battle raged. The Roland came back for a second attempt but Bott's pilot spurred the nimble Sopwith around and used full throttle to charge at the now converging enemy, blazing away with his forward-firing gun.

At barely 50 yards it was the German who blinked first and sheered away. The Sopwith gave chase still pumping rounds from the pilot's machine gun. Satisfyingly a streak of flame belched from the Roland's fuel tank and down he went. There were more, another pair of single-seaters fastened onto the Sopwith, Bott still frantically trying to clear the jam. Rounds punched through the thin fuselage around him. At last he freed the breech, banged home the drum and joined the fight.

One of the Rolands came broadside on across the Sopwith's tail so Bott cut loose with a full magazine, raking the enemy from stem to stern. Despite the amount of lead he was spitting at virtually point-blank range the Roland sailed on serenely; though he may in fact have been significantly damaged, as he took no further part in the combat. The remaining German pilot clearly thought so as he turned tail and fled.

During the whole Somme battle, the primary role of the RFC was reconnaissance and spotting. This was vital and to achieve it the Allies needed control of the skies. This was dearly bought. Trenchard (commander of the RFC) pursued an aggressive policy, ready to accept high casualties to win the skies. Losses were indeed high but would have been worse if so many German aircraft had not been diverted south to Verdun. Nonetheless, the RFC did brilliant work as the eyes of the BEF. Their BE2c planes could be fitted with wireless which enabled the observer to guide shells onto target, using a straightforward clock-code for corrections.

Control of the skies

The RFC was beginning to win ground over the Western Front in that hot summer of 1916. Manufacturing output had increased exponentially and there was no shortage of recruits. What they did not have were purpose-built engines – the Royal Aircraft Establishment had to rely on whatever the French had left over. These mainly went into the new DH2. This was another 'pusher', virtually obsolete before it ever flew, soon christened the 'spinning incinerator' by crews. It did, for a while at least, seem to even the odds. The forward-firing Lewis had a good field of fire and, as it didn't need an interrupter mechanism, a higher rate of shooting. The Sopwith Pups mainly went to the RNAS. RFC pilots yearned to get their hands on a Nieuport 17.

Captain Harold Wylie of 23 Squadron was flying a DH2 'pusher'. Jumped by a posse of Eindeckers who had shot off Very lights to signal the charge, the attackers became wary after the first pass. One of the British flyers was shot down, another had his observer killed outright, though not before he'd fatally damaged the Fokker. Wylie's own observer, Powell, was blazing away as a German round grazed his trigger finger then glanced off into his eye. He fell back, probably already dead, breaking a leg. Wylie, now without armament, was badly shot up but somehow managed to land the plane and walk away.

Trenchard's aggressive ethos was adopted by the flyers who considered no odds too great. Lieutenant W. O. Tudor-Hart and a Captain Webb from 22 Squadron were some five miles into bandit country flying an FE2b when they spotted eight enemy machines coming in from the south-west. The British immediately attacked. Tudor-Hart was the gunner and gave the first two a burst as they came overhead at about 300 yards. He signalled that Webb should bank so he could get a better shot but Webb put the plane into a glide. Why was soon obvious – he'd been hit in the stomach and died over his joystick in seconds.

Tudor-Hart had to try and steer the aircraft while constantly ducking back to the gun to loose off a burst. He struggled to get the plane pointing in the general direction of Allied lines before taking on the slew of enemy now circling. As he couldn't move his dead comrade he had to steer with his hand over the wind-shield. Tudor-Hart didn't expect to survive himself but was determined to make a fight of it as the plane hobbled back towards safety.

It was probably the very bizarre, erratic course of the plane which saved him. Eventually he descended to tree height. He was still behind enemy lines and he could plainly see infantry covering his descent with rifles. He realised even if he got down safely, he'd not have time to set the aircraft on fire. He wasn't about to offer the Germans a free gift so he deliberately went in nose down. The plane was a write-off. Miraculously he wasn't – suffering much bruising, one busted rib and ankle.

Immelmann's demise and then Boelcke's marked the passing of the Fokker scourge. It still wasn't safe for the Allies in the skies though. Germany had a new aerial paladin. Boelcke's old pupil Manfred von Richthofen had risen to fill the vacancy of ace of aces. He had a new machine to help him earn his deadly

Air Marshal Hugh Montague Trenchard, 1st Viscount Trenchard GCB OM GCVO DSO (1873–1956) was the senior British officer who commanded the RFC and was instrumental in establishing the Royal Air Force. He has been described as the 'Father of the Royal Air Force'. His policy of unremitting offensive cost the lives of hundreds of pilots under-equipped with inferior aircraft.

reputation; the Albatros D series. This was a variant of the earlier two-seaters, powered by a hefty 160 hp water-cooled Mercedes engine. It could fly higher and faster and its twin machine guns doubled the rate of fire. It was another game-changer. The Sopwith 1½ strutters were instantly outclassed as were all Allied fighters.

Major Lanoe Hawker VC, DSO was the British *beau sabreur*. Like his soon-to-be nemesis he was a hunter, though he had transferred from the Royal Engineers. He'd rigged up a .30 calibre Westley Richards stalking rifle on a bespoke mount which acted as an outrigger to clear his propeller. He flew like a ballerina and struck like a serpent. Rifles might be yesterday's weapon in the air but he used his to deadly effect. Germans fell to his front-mounted Lewis gun but the single lethal shot claimed a few more. So sure, so deft was his touch, like a Borgia assassin he'd manoeuvre to send that one round through an enemy's brain or his engine – either would be fatal.

His policy was one of *à outrance* – all-out aggression. He had designed a better clamping mechanism for the Lewis gun in his DH2; he'd also designed warmer, thigh-length, sheepskin flying boots. The Albatros completely outclassed the British 'pusher' and very quickly made its presence felt. Hawker himself survived several near misses. Like all aces, he became the 'must-kill' target for young bucks in the hungry new *jastas*. The RNAS was beginning to get newer and better planes such as the Sopwith Pup and Triplane but Hawker's 24 Squadron were stuck with the lumbering DH2s, those who survived anyway.

On 16 November 1916, pursuing an attack on German machines, Hawker, his wingman out of action, found himself up against von Richthofen, a duel of titans. But a very unequal one, the DH2 was an antique by comparison. The fight which followed was drawn out, tortuous and nerve shredding. The rising German ace made sure he never offered his adversary a steady target. They circled like mongoose and cobra, one strike would be enough, life and death.

As the infantry below, dirty, wet, exhausted and lice-ridden, watched the show above, the two flyers executed a brilliant series of turns, each seeking the advantage. Hawker was heading for Allied lines and safety, von Richthofen was determined he'd never arrive. Hawker's magical touch enabled him to side-slip at the apex of the turn, frustrating the greater speed and power of the Albatros. He swooped and dived, turned and jinked. But you can only dive so far till you run out of airspace.

After perhaps twenty minutes both planes were very low indeed, Hawker nearly clipping the trees, narrowly dodging chimney stacks and rooftops, von Richthofen like a terrier on his tail. Pockets of air would lift the DH2 like a magic carpet and give him a few hundred more feet of sky to work with. Von Richthofen was about 60 metres away as Hawker struggled to make the final turn, one which would swing him about to meet his tormentor face to face and which might just be enough. It wasn't, the nimble Albatros surged forward like a tiger, guns blazing, raking Hawker's plane.

One round took off the back of the Englishman's head and his plane spun down to burst into flames on impact. This was just south of Bapoume – it was German soldiers who recovered what was left and buried him nearby. Von Richthofen recovered the twisted Lewis gun from Hawker's plane as a trophy and they say he hung it above the entrance to his billet. L. 24G. Hawker has no known grave and is commemorated on the Arras Memorial. Von Richthofen called him the 'British Boelcke'. As flying obituaries go, that's high praise indeed.

CHAPTER 2

BLOODY APRIL

1917–18

I am a hunter. My brother Lothar is a butcher. When I have shot down an Englishman my hunting passion is satisfied for a quarter of an hour.

Manfred von Richthofen

HE WAS THE PERFECT ACE; A born, obsessive hunter, remorseless, friendless, a brilliant instructor but always a loner who showed affection to none, other than his dog Moritz. The hound used to accompany him in the cockpit; every hunter needs a dog. By the time of his death, with 82 credited kills, he was, by Great War aviation standards, an old man, all of 25, the same age as Hawker had been when he killed him.

The British strategy of pushing patrols over the German lines suited him perfectly, like driven game; 'it is better if the customers come to the shop'. He wasn't given to showing too much respect for adversaries, be these Anglo Saxon: 'Certainly they are brave, but it is bravery that has a touch of foolishness about it', or Gallic: 'In a Frenchman bravery is quite exceptional and if you do meet it, it is like a glass of lemonade and very soon goes flat'. This was the man who, more than any other, would come to symbolise the epitome of the ace. 'The Red Baron's' glamour would outlast the war and perhaps even today, he remains the perfect example of the breed.

1917: Year of circuses

The carnage of the Somme and Verdun had taught the Allies new tricks, far better gunnery and the creeping emergence of the armoured leviathan that is the tank as a potential arbiter on the battlefield. There were moments of hope in 1917. The British achieved remarkable gains on the first day of the battle of Arras in April and General Plumber won a stunning victory at Messines in June, showing how it might be done. But it wasn't done during the third battle of Ypres. French General Robert Nivelle bungled his botched offensive and thousands of *poilus* decided they'd had just enough of incompetent butchers. So did the Russians. The battle of Cambrai in November/December foreshadowed the shape of things to come but, all considered, it wasn't a vintage year.

As 1917 opened and spring offensives loomed, the Allies still didn't have an effective competitor for the latest variant of the hugely successful Albatros. This was the DIII, with its bigger engine and more advanced 'V-Strutter' wing design. With two belt-fed, synchronised machine guns, these new Albatros fighters packed a terrific punch. Although the new wing design had some inherent structural weaknesses and an occasional penchant for the wing to sheer off, the Allies had nothing that came near.

As a prelude to the Arras offensive General Allenby, commanding Third Army, was to lead in April, intensive reconnaissance was needed. That meant, as ever, taking the fight to the Germans. As ever, the Germans could afford to wait – the customers were still coming to the shop. There were 37 *jastas* stationed on the Western Front that late winter/spring. They could climb into the sun, safe behind their own lines and wait like hawks to pounce. The vulnerable two-seaters, even the nippier Sopwith 1½ strutter, were easy meat.

The British offensive at Arras was essentially a diversion – intended to pin German forces down while Robert Nivelle delivered his major blow along the Aisne. Arras was a limited but very costly success. Nivelle's great punch smacked into empty air and cost the French yet more casualties. It was at this point the *poilus* decided they had had enough. The RFC never did, though their losses were terrible, the worst in the entire span of the conflict. Veterans and novices were lost in great numbers, the former irreplaceable; the latter's lifespan often measured in days.

'Bloody April' witnessed the loss of over nine hundred British airmen; Manfred von Richthofen accounted for 21 of these, by far his best single month. Richthofen's diary describes the events of one of those April days:

The second of April, 1917, was a very warm day for my Squadron. From my quarters I could clearly hear the drum-fire of the guns which was again particularly violent. I was still in bed when my orderly rushed into the room and exclaimed: 'Sir, the English are here!' Sleepy as I was, I looked out of the window and, really, there were my dear friends circling over the flying ground. I jumped out of my bed and into my clothes in a jiffy. My Red Bird had been pulled out and was ready for starting. My mechanics knew that I should probably not allow such a favourable moment to go by un-utilized. Everything was ready. I snatched up my furs and then went off.

I was the last to start. My comrades were much nearer to the enemy. I feared that my prey would escape me, that I should have to look on from a distance while the others were fighting. Suddenly one of the impertinent fellows tried to drop down upon me. I allowed him to come near and then we started a merry quadrille. Sometimes my opponent flew on his back and sometimes he did other tricks. He had a double-seated chaser. I was his master and very soon I recognized that he could not escape me.

During an interval in the fighting I convinced myself that we were alone. It followed that the victory would accrue to him who was calmest, who shot best and who had the clearest brain in a moment of danger. After a short time I got him beneath me without seriously hurting him with my gun. We were at least two kilometres from the front.

I thought he intended to land but there I had made a mistake. Suddenly, when he was only a few yards above the ground, he once more went off on a straight course. He tried to escape me. That was too bad. I attacked him again and I went so low that I feared I should touch the roofs of the houses of the village beneath me. The Englishman defended himself up to the last moment. At the very end I felt that my engine had been hit. Still I did not let go. He had to fall. He rushed at full speed right into a block of houses.

There was little left to be done. This was once more a case of splendid daring. He defended himself to the last. However, in my opinion he showed more foolhardiness than courage. This was one of the cases where one must differentiate between energy and idiocy. He had to come down in any case but he paid for his stupidity with his life.

I was delighted with the performance of my red machine during its morning work and returned to our quarters. My comrades were still in the air and they were very surprised, when, as we met at breakfast, I told them that I had scored my thirty-second machine.

A very young Lieutenant had 'bagged' his first airplane. We were all very merry and prepared everything for further battles. I then went and groomed myself. I had not had time to do it previously. I was visited by a dear friend, Lieutenant Voss of Boelcke's Squadron. We chatted. Voss had downed on the previous day his twenty-third machine. He was next to me on the list and is at present my most redoubtable competitor.

When he started to fly home I offered to accompany him part of the way. We went on a roundabout way over the Fronts. The weather had turned so bad that we could not hope to find any more game.

Beneath us there were dense clouds. Voss did not know the country and he began to feel uncomfortable. When we passed above Arras I met my brother who also is in my squadron and who had lost his way. He joined us. Of course he recognized me at once by the colour of my machine.

Suddenly we saw a squadron approaching from the other side. Immediately the thought occurred to me: 'Now comes number thirty-three.' Although there were nine Englishmen and although they were on their own territory they preferred to avoid battle. I thought that perhaps it would be better for me to re-paint my machine. Nevertheless we caught them up. The important thing in aircraft is that they are speedy.

I was nearest to the enemy and attacked the man to the rear. To my greatest delight I noticed that he accepted battle and my pleasure was increased when I discovered that his comrades deserted him. So I had once more a single fight. It was a fight similar to the one which I had had in the morning. My opponent did not make matters easy for me. He knew the fighting business and it was particularly awkward for me that he was a good shot. To my great regret that was quite clear to me.

A favourable wind came to my aid. It drove both of us into the German lines. My opponent discovered that the matter was not so simple as he had imagined. So he plunged and disappeared in a cloud. He had nearly saved himself.

I plunged after him and dropped out of the cloud and, as luck would have it, found myself close behind him. I fired and he fired without any tangible result. At last I hit him. I noticed a ribbon of white benzene vapour. He had to land for his engine had come to a stop.

He was a stubborn fellow. He was bound to recognize that he had lost the game. If he continued shooting I could kill him, for meanwhile we had dropped to an altitude of about nine hundred feet. However, the Englishman defended himself exactly as did his countryman in the morning. He fought until he landed. When he had come to the ground I flew over him at an altitude of about thirty feet in order to ascertain whether I had killed him or not. What did the rascal do? He took his machine-gun and shot holes into my machine.

Afterwards Voss told me if that had happened to him he would have shot the airman on the ground. As a matter of fact I ought to have done so for he had not surrendered. He was one of the few fortunate fellows who escaped with their lives. I felt very merry, flew home and celebrated my thirty-third aeroplane.

The one small ray of light on the Allied horizon was the arrival of the new Sopwith Triplane. It could climb like an eagle and manoeuvre like a sparrowhawk. These new fighters went to the RNAS who passed their retiring Spads on to the RFC. As the body count rocketed, the army requested the navy send at least one squadron of 'Tripehounds' south to the battle zone. The

A Sopwith F-1 Camel. (USAF)

Admiralty sent No 10 Squadron and the effect was immediate. The new planes so impressed their German adversaries, manufacturers were queuing up to start building.

Though potentially a game-changer, the Tripehounds were never produced in sufficient numbers – only 140 in total. The Sopwith Pup, Spad VII and Nieuport 17 were all outclassed. Rushed into production was the new SE5. Early trials were unpromising, the aircraft had significant failings but the SE5A proved one of the best fighters of the war. It was fast and agile enough and mounted two machine guns though one was a wing-mounted Lewis, an excellent gun platform. The equally new and potent Spad XIII was another weapon in the revitalised Allied arsenal. This mounted twin Vickers on the fuselage and so could compete directly with the best of the Albatros fighters.

These new planes arrived in late spring and were followed in July by the legendary Sopwith Camel – arguably the best of all Allied fighters. This was a direct descendant of the Pup, still with a rotary engine. It too mounted twin Vickers and performed like a virtuoso trapeze artist. The Germans had grown complacent, the ascendancy of the Albatros DIII seemed so assured but its days were numbered and the DV had to be rushed into production. However, it was only a marginal improvement on its predecessor. Even the famous Fokker Triplane was already sinking into obsolescence but it remained very agile and very well armed. It became the aircraft of the elite German aces, becoming nearly as famous as von Richthofen himself.

It wasn't all about the planes – tactics were changing. The old days of lone aces prowling the skies like Achilles on wings were on the way out. The scale of the air war like that on land was increasing exponentially. The fighter squadron, *jasta* and *escadrille de chasse* formed a new order. As more planes took to the sky the Germans, always outnumbered, took to forming ad hoc fighter wings or *jagdgeschwader*. Von Richthofen was appointed to lead the first of these at the start of June. Comprising four squadrons, this was a mobile force that could be shunted along the line to counter any major threat, to achieve local supremacy when it really mattered. His command became the first of the 'flying circuses' and the concept proved a very effective remedy.

The **F2A and F2B**, the Bristol fighter that was in fact a two-seater came in during March 1917. It was impressive, another game changer with a hefty 275 hp Rolls-Royce Falcon III engine. It worked for reconnaissance, as a scout and bomber. British designers were finally gaining an edge. On 30 November, a lone Bristol fighter from 11 Squadron, crewed by Lieutenant McKeever and Sergeant Powell took on a German formation of nine and accounted for four of them.

Replica of von Richthofen's red Fokker Triplane.

The French often tended to bunch their star pilots into specific, elite squadrons like Les Cigognes and Les Sportifs. The British preferred not to, they did not really care for the whole celebrity business though British aces such as Billy Bishop, James McCudden and Mick Mannock did enjoy immense popularity. This meant air battles would get bigger though still not on the scale of 1918 when aerial warfare really came of age.

Plans were afoot to establish Britain's air arm as a discrete force, though the Royal Air Force would not come into being until 1 April 1918; this was the shape of things to come. In part, this was a response to the bomber raids now hitting southern England. Worse, from the German perspective, the United States declared war on 6 April and this meant time was running out. Germany was close to victory in the east but with the Americans in the war, the odds in the west would finally tilt too far. Though the high command overestimated America at this stage, plans for the grand knockout blow were already in hand.

Aces high

The sheer intensity and scale of the air war in early 1917 surpassed anything the pioneers of 1914 could even have dreamed of, or possibly had nightmares about. During the spring battles a new RFC subaltern enjoyed a life expectancy of 11 days. Life in the mess was boisterous as ever, doubts and fears were not allowed. Alone in their fevered cots men sweated and wept. The strains were unbearable.

Some began visibly to crack – 'poor old B; caught it yesterday, down in flames over Menin. He had been acting strange for the last few days, wandering about speaking to himself' (Cecil Lewis). There were no mechanisms for not coping. It was stiff upper lips all round. Many found excuses to return early from patrol, jammed guns, real or arranged, could come in handy. Men had terrible nightmares reliving the moment a comrade burned to death or took the second option of jumping to his death. The press was far hungrier for glory than reality, that wasn't at all what folks back home wanted to read about.

Georges Marie Ludovic Jules Guynemer came from impeccable aristocratic stock. Sickly as a child he was initially rejected for military service as unfit but managed to get in as a mechanic, hardly the role his heritage had prepared him for. But he had grit and pushed hard for pilot training. His persistence worked and in June 1915 he was posted to Escadrille MS.3 – as it was to become. His first plane was a fairly venerable Morane-Saulnier I Monoplane named *Vieux Charles* after a previous owner. Still, it was good enough and he brought down an Aviatik. He kept the name – it appeared lucky – even when his squadron was re-branded and issued with Nieuport 17s. By February 1916, he was officially an 'ace' with five confirmed kills.

He was commissioned as a lieutenant in March and by Christmas had downed 25 Germans. His commander of the Escadrille N3 (known as the 'Storks') called him the best of the breed. Very soon Guynemer had taken over leadership of the squadron,

Georges Guynemer, 1917.

now the ultra-elite Cigognes. His influence grew and a press hungry for heroes promoted him to celebrity status. He was of sufficient stature to influence Spad's design of the XII and XIII. He'd been critical of the current model though he'd become the first Allied ace to dispatch a German Gotha bomber while flying one.

Though the RFC bled in spring 1917, Guynemer had a very good May with seven confirmed kills. He was now flying the Spad XII and had upped its firepower with a bespoke 37mm cannon that fired through the propeller shaft. This was the shape of things to come but it was not without its eccentricities. It was single shot and had to be reloaded manually every time, the breech interfered with the controls and the recoil seriously impeded the plane's speed. With every round it belched out a foul cloud of smoke. Still he used this fearsome ordnance to very good effect, shooting down two more enemy at the end of July. He was the first French ace to rack up a score of 50.

Photos of Guynemer in 1917 show a man who looks much older than his years. One has to wonder: combat fatigue and post-traumatic stress disorder were denied but their effects were very real. A breakdown could get you sectioned or, at worst, an appointment with the firing squad. In the picture Guynemer is thin to the point of emaciation with the haunted eyes of the 'thousand yard stare'. His ranked rows of decorations almost seem a mockery. He had survived the intensity of Verdun and was pitched into the northerly skies of Flanders to assist the RFC supporting General Plumer's Second Army and the battle for

Messines. When he came home for a full three days leave his father begged him to step back into a non-combat role. But his son had become a slave to his own legend. Guynemer couldn't leave while the fight was still on. He had to carry on even though the road to Ypres surely led to the grave. His adoring public would have seen him as a quitter, one who had reaped the spoils then slunk off. He was at the limit of man's endurance but his unequivocal view was that limits only exist to be exceeded – 'unless you give all, you give nothing'. Perhaps this was in part bravado, almost vanity, and yet Guynemer showed that sublime courage, that almost willingness to sacrifice all that marks out the true ace.

On 11 September 1917 he took off for the last time. The week had gone badly, a series of mechanical ills had unsettled everyone – airmen were notoriously superstitious. He was flying a Spad XIII over Langemarck in the Ypres Salient. At 09.25, he detected a lone German Rumpler two-seater. His wingman was a rookie and by the time he'd got clear of the overhead fighter escort, his chief had vanished. He was never seen again.

Over a week later a captured German flyer recalled hearing an infantry sergeant who'd been on the scene when Guynemer came down. He was stone dead; shot clean through the head. A burial detail was formed but shellfire drove them back from the wreck. His end, fittingly perhaps, remains an enigma. One of his fellow pilots, who took part in the final mission, left this account:

> Guynemer sighted five machines of the Albatros type D-3. Without hesitation, he bore down on them. At that moment enemy patrolling machines, soaring at a great height, appeared suddenly and fell upon Guynemer. There were forty enemy machines in the air at this time, including Baron von Richthofen and his circus division of machines, painted in diagonal blue and white stripes. Toward Guynemer's right some Belgian machines hove in sight, but it was too late. Guynemer must have been hit. His machine dropped gently toward the earth, and I lost track of it. All that I can say is that the machine was not on fire.

Some extra details were furnished by his commander, Major Brocard, and subsequently published in *Le Matin*:

> The last fight of the French aviator occurred four or five miles inside the German lines northeast of Ypres and opposite the British lines. Captain Guynemer was accompanied by Lieutenant Bozon Verduraz, who says that they were flying at a height of 15,000 feet when Guynemer sighted an enemy two-seater, which he attacked. Almost at the same moment Verduraz saw four German monoplanes approaching and turned toward them instantly so as to draw them off. They circled around for a while and then disappeared. Verduraz then returned to the place where he had left Guynemer engaged with the German biplane, but Guynemer had vanished.

The American Red Cross was later to add further detail:

> … Guynemer was shot through the head north of Poelcapelle, on the Ypres front. His body was identified by a photograph on his pilot's license found in his pocket. The burial took place at Brussels in the presence of a guard of honor, composed of the 5th Prussian Division. Such is the story told by a Belgian, who has just escaped from the Germans. The burial was about to take place at Poelcapelle, when the bombardment preceding the British attack at Ypres started. The burying party hastily withdrew, taking the body with them. The German General chanced to be an aviation enthusiast with a great admiration for Captain Guynemer's achievements.
>
> At his direction the body was taken to Brussels in a special funeral car. Thither the captain was carried by non-commissioned officers and was covered with floral tributes from German aviators. The Prussian Guards stood at salute upon its arrival and during the burial, which was given all possible military honors. The French Government has been invited to place in the Pantheon, where many great Frenchmen are buried, an inscription to perpetuate the memory of Captain Guynemer as 'a symbol of the aspirations and enthusiasm of the Army.' A resolution to this effect has been introduced in the Chamber of Deputies by Deputy Lasies.

Albert Ball was dead at 20 but by then he had received the Victoria Cross, Distinguished Service Order and two bars, and the Military Cross. Of all the British aces he, perhaps more than any, even McCudden and Mannock, typified the spirit of the RFC. Unlike Guynemer, he was born and raised a working-class boy in Nottingham. He enlisted in August 1914 and served with the 2/7th (Robin Hood) Battalion of the Sherwood Foresters. He rose rapidly to become an NCO and was commissioned before the end of the year. Moved to a training role, he soon chafed and transferred out of the Foresters to a cyclist battalion but the posting to France and action still eluded him.

It was in 1915 that he took private flying lessons at Hendon, the Ruffy-Baumann school. It was an expensive business at £75–£100, which equates to say £8,000–£10,000 in today's money. He would be up at 03.00 to bike to the aerodrome for a lesson before getting back in time for reveille at 06.45. His boyish good looks meant that, aside from being very popular with girls, he had just the style the press would later seek out.

Never one to be blinded by sentiment, he accepted the lottery of death that flying offered. Getting killed was always a potential park of the package: 'Yesterday a ripping boy had a smash, and when we got up to him he was nearly dead, he had a two-inch piece of wood right through his head and died this morning. If you would like a flight I should be pleased to take you any time you wish…' We don't know whether the recipient took Ball up on his offer.

Ball qualified on 15 October 1915 but he'd yet to fully earn his wings. He requested and got a transfer to the RFC though he still wasn't getting as far as France. He underwent more training at Mousehold Heath near Norfolk. Up to now, his instructors didn't rate him above average. His first solo effort in a Maurice Farman, the venerable Longhorn, went rather bumpily. No pushover, he rounded on the instructor who quipped about the dodgy landing, after all he'd only had a quarter of an hour's practice with the plane. He finally earned the coveted wings and formally transferred to the RFC.

It was on 18 February 1916 when he finally flew to France and the scent of cordite, assigned to 13 Squadron at Marieux. He started his active service flying a two-seater BE2c in a reconnaissance role. It was an exciting baptism. Shot down on 27 March but returning to the air undeterred, he and his observer Lieutenant Villiers were soon routinely swapping lead with German planes. Already getting recognised for his aggressive spirit, Ball was getting into his stride, though in his letters home he discouraged his younger brother from joining the RFC.

Soon, he was given one of the coveted single-seaters, a Bristol Scout. In May 1916, he transferred to 11 Squadron which flew Scouts, Nieuport 16s and FE2b pushers. He was interested in engineering and what made his plane fly. Some more dilettante officers preferred to leave the tradesman's work to their mechanics but not Ball. Like McCudden he realised that performance, reliability and punch were the keys to survival. He was fastidious; finding his quarters uncongenial and dirty, he built his own complete with miniature garden.

Albert Ball was the classic ace of that phase of the war. Something of a loner, never a 'team player', he stalked his prey relentlessly. His preferred attack was to approach from below, taking advantage of the enemy's blind quarter then angle upwards to fire a burst from his wing-mounted Lewis gun. In technical terms this was a tricky manoeuvre.

On the ground he adopted a slightly rakish air, more at home playing his violin than roistering in the mess. He was always his own mechanic and didn't boast any level of sartorial elegance. Perhaps his only vanity was his Byronic hair which regularly escaped the squadron barber for rather longer than the rules allowed. On 11 May he finally scored, forcing down an enemy two-seater. He upgraded from a Scout to a Nieuport and his tally began to rise; two LVGs on 29 May, an Eindecker two days later. On 25 June be shot down a German balloon and racked up five victories – officially now an ace.

That hot summer he flew BE2s with 8 Squadron. On 28 July, he undertook a daring mission to fly a French agent over the lines. This was the sort of clandestine work the Westland Lysander would become famous for in the next war, ferrying SOE and resistors. Ball's flight was something of a first and it proved exciting, a trio of Fokkers hot on his tail. When they did land safely the panicked agent initially refused to get out of the plane. It was during his time with 8 Squadron that Ball won his Military Cross. This was awarded for bravery on numerous occasions, but particularly in one scrap where he'd torn heedlessly into six of the enemy. But that was Ball. He embodied that spirit of reckless gallantry combined with all the skills and patience of the true hunter.

On the day he reached 20, Ball was promoted to captain. On 22 August he knocked down three Roland C11s in a single flight and rounded it off by taking on 14 enemy single handed. His plane thoroughly shot up, he just struggled back to Allied lines. Soon he was flying with 60 Squadron and, as a star flyer, was given carte blanche; he was a unit within a unit, his own plane and support team. With his red propeller boss he proclaimed his individual status. Albert Ball, the lad from Nottinghamshire, had finally arrived.

And Nottingham loved him, he was the local celebrity. Amid the stringencies of the home front, the fear of Zeppelins and those ever-mounting casualty lists crowding the newspapers, folk had something to shout about. He was mobbed in his home town and the government, initially suspicious of 'celeb' status, woke up to its propaganda value. Back in France he added rockets to the arsenal of his Nieuport which significantly disconcerted a trio of Roland CIIIs. Then he moved up to the Nieuport 17, customised to be tail heavy to make changing the ammo drum on the wing-mounted Lewis easier. Knocking down three enemy in a day became a habit. By the end of September his score stood at 31.

These victories, the constant strain of flying aggressive patrols, inevitably took its toll. By October 1916 he was in urgent need of R&R. By now he'd now earned his DSO and bar, awarded simultaneously, together with the Russian Order of St George. Back home he was a real hero, the press were all over him. His leave became an extended photo opportunity. On 18 November, the young man from Nottingham, once labelled an indifferent pilot, was at Buckingham Palace to receive his medals. Subsequently he earned a second bar to his DSO – the first to receive the award three times.

After his leave he didn't return immediately to France. Instead he was posted to training duties with a reserve squadron in Suffolk. He used the time to focus on his own design – the Austin-Ball AFB1 fighter. This didn't reach the front until after his final mission. But he did get to fly the prototype SE5 and like others, wasn't impressed. Though the plane was to be much improved, his scepticism endured.

Ball met rising stars James McCudden and Billy Bishop (who wasn't blooded at this stage). He also met Flora Young, who accepted his invitation to fly with him and latterly, on 5 April 1917, his proposal of marriage. He needed to be back in the action and lobbied to return to France. He was assigned as a flight commander to 56 Squadron. The unit was being equipped with SE5s but he preferred to cling to his Nieuport 17 – for solo missions at least, on patrol he would fly the new plane. Such eccentricities went against the grain, though Trenchard, perhaps grudgingly, acquiesced.

Once he got his SE5 (no. A4850) out of its packing crates, he began his habitual customisation. He stripped off the forward-firing Vickers and installed a second Lewis gun, angled to fire downwards through a new gun-port in the floor of the cockpit. The new kit was soon tested. On 23 April that bloody spring he flew five sorties, killed an Albatros, had his Nieuport shot up, struggled back to base, took off in the SE5, had to land to clear a jammed gun then came back, bagged another Albatros and shot up a two-seater.

As the fighting at Arras continued, Ball was more than doing his bit to ensure the German air service was having a bloody spring of its own. He kept on racking them up, though his plane had to be sent for refurbishment – it had taken so much punishment. On 5 May he knocked down two DIIIs. One of these had come straight at him, a screaming head-on storm of lead. He had done for the pilot but his oil tank took a hit and he was blinded by spurting gouts. Oil pressure totally gone, he barely limped back. Even nerves of steel fray after a while and he was well into overdraft.

He still flew the redoubtable Nieuport on solo hunts but this was no longer the fine sport it had been. The Germans were learning to fight in packs and didn't offer as many tempting individual targets any more. Billy Bishop was now at the front and, flying in on the evening of 6 May, Ball suggested a joint raid to beat up Von Richthofen's Flying Circus at dawn, catching the prey on the ground. Bishop agreed but the stunt was to be delayed until after his forthcoming leave.

Next evening, 7 May, 56 Squadron and Jasta 11 scrapped in an evening sky with darkening visibility; the bright firefly aircraft wheeled and spat. Cecil Lewis was one of those who saw Ball chase after Lothar von Richthofen's bright red DIII. The German ace made it back, Ball didn't. He disappeared into cloud and never officially emerged. One German officer on the ground witnessed his plane spinning earthwards with a busted prop. Leutnant Hailer and his squad rushed to reach the wrecked plane. Ball, though certainly dead, was taken to a nearby field hospital. He appears to have died from injuries sustained in the crash, he had no wounds.

The German high command was quick to assert he had been brought down by Lothar but this seems unlikely. Mechanical or pilot error was almost certainly the cause. He was buried in the cemetery at Annoeullin with full honours. The enemy dubbed him the 'English Richthofen'. And, it was they who inscribed the cross '*In Luftkampf gefallen für sein Vaterland Engl. Flieger Hauptmann Albert Ball, Royal Flying Corps*' (Fallen in air combat for his fatherland English pilot Captain Albert Ball). He was awarded a posthumous Victoria Cross and a sell-out memorial service was held in his parish church of St Mary's in Nottingham.

Dying doesn't necessarily inhibit an ace's popularity – far from it. Ball is probably more famous than his pal Bishop who also went on to win a Victoria Cross, score 72 kills and live to die in his bed. René Fonck, 'ace of aces' with 75 victories who also survived, never quite had the allure of Guynemer. The last year of the war would be a bad one for the air aces, not just the attrition rate which stayed high, but in the changing nature of aerial warfare.

1918: Year of decision

Elijah was reputed to be the patron saint of aviators, but as he went to Heaven in a chariot of fire, this was something we weren't too keen about.

Kiffin Yates Rockwell, US pilot who claimed the first American 'kill' of World War I

With the United States in the war, Germany was running out of time. She'd beaten Russia, carving out huge gains in the east but these would turn to ashes without victory in the west. Ludendorff's legions hammered the Allies, punching great wedges of salient into the lines but never breaking them. Then, like a spring tide, they ran out of momentum, elite storm troopers mostly used up. The British offensive at Amiens on 8 August was the 'black day' of the Imperial army – it was downhill from there to the armistice in November. And then finally, at 11.00 on the 11th day of the 11th month the monstrous anger of the guns suddenly subsided. The world would never be the same again, neither on the ground nor in the air.

Even von Richthofen, the greatest ace of all, wasn't immortal. Wounded in the head he took sick leave from September to November 1917. Though he returned to flying duty and would bring down another 23 Allied aircraft, something of the fire had gone out of him. Besides, at 25, he was an old man.

The potential arrival of the Americans, even though their capacity at the outset was very limited, spurred General Ernst Wilhelm von Hoeppner to rethink strategy for 1918. He planned to create another 40 fighter units and 17 army liaison squadrons.

This meant Germany, desperately short of everything: raw materials, supplies, skilled workers and recruits, would somehow have to build 2,000 new aircraft every week. He would need 24,000 new trainees. The war was crucifying Germany and the British blockade was threatening to starve an already hungry populace.

Trenchard was aware the enemy was raising his game yet again but remained adamant that the primary role of the RFC (soon to be the Royal Air Force, RAF) was to act as the eyes and ears of the army. Once enemy build-up was detected and the supporting supply lines and infrastructure identified, then the flyers would move into their secondary role – coordinating artillery fire and bombing everything in sight, strafing the ground and generally creating as much mayhem as possible. Beating up enemy infantry formations was another key role. This was the beginning of full ground and air cooperation that

Ernst Wilhelm von Hoeppner (1860–1922) was a cavalryman who held a series of senior appointments in the early years of World War I before being given command of the disparate elements of the German air service in 1916. He reported directly to Hindenburg, the Chief of General Staff, and held the substantive rank of lieutenant general. The expansion and re-ordering of the air service was his brainchild and he was awarded a Blue Max, even though he never flew – a fact some junior officers resented!

would certainly facilitate the Allied victories won during the last hundred days.

None of this could occur unless the RFC first controlled the skies. In terms of the overall offensive spirit it was very much business as usual; attack, attack, and keep on attacking. The previous year had been hard on aces, both Allied and German. The deadly Werner Voss had scored 48 kills before he finally went down in an epic brawl above what was left of Ypres on 23 September. Von Richthofen and his brother Lothar were among the few to keep going. Manfred, the star pupil of his mentor Boelcke, was an equally passionate and dedicated instructor. His doctrine, straight from the master, was brutally simple: 'I approach the enemy from behind to within 50 metres. I aim carefully, fire and the enemy falls. ... One does not need to be a clever pilot, or a crack shot, one only needs the courage to fly in close to the enemy before opening fire.'

One of the new rising stars who came under his wing was Ernst Udet. Born in 1896, Udet had come up through the infantry, flown two-seaters then made it into a fighter with Jasta 15 in September 1916. He won six victories and rose to command

Ernst Udet (1896–1941) survived World War I, scoring 62 victories. He joined the Nazi Party in 1933. An acquaintance of Göring, he became director of research and development for the Luftwaffe. He was heavily involved in the design of the Ju 87 – Stuka dive-bomber, though drink and disillusionment drove him to suicide in 1941. There were persistent rumours after his death that he had actually been murdered on the orders of the high command because he had become 'unreliable'.

Ernst Udet.

Mick Mannock VC in flying gear.

the squadron but was drawn by the gilded allure of Richthofen's flying circus Jagdgeschwader 1. He wasn't disappointed. Von Richthofen, like Boelcke before him, was such a titan that he should probably have been kept safe somewhere. But like Guynemer and Ball and all those others, he could never sit it out while others fought. He 'would hold his manhood cheap' if he had simply sat back resting on his laurels while others flew the dawn patrol; while every humble Fritz in the trenches went on fighting because the luxury of retirement was not on offer.

After Ball's death Britain had no von Richthofen as both top ace and tactical inspiration. They did have Mick Mannock though, another who would go on to receive the Victoria Cross. Not a natural ace perhaps and, at 30 in 1918, a very old man indeed. In 1914, he'd been working as a telephone engineer in Turkey, returning home to join up and fight his former employers. He served first with the Royal Engineers and then with Royal Army Medical Corps before transferring to the RFC in 1916.

His early career in the skies during 1917 with 40 Squadron showed no great promise. A deeply introverted man, there were those who suspected he was windy or faint-hearted perhaps.

They were to learn differently. He was to emerge as a sound tactician, analytical, cautious, the very opposite to a lone wolf such as Ball. He stressed the need for professionalism within a team environment. Ira Jones was a great admirer:

> On 30th April 1917 Mick took me up to 'see me right' as he put it. Near Poperinghe, we spotted a Hun two-seater. Instead of signalling for me to go down with him, he told me to stay where I was. All signals are given by hand-movements and moving the aircraft in various ways. By this time we were circling around the Hun and had the sun behind us. When we were almost directly ahead of the Hun, down goes Mick like a rocket; he positioned himself so that the pilot could not see him because of the upper wing, and the observer was looking the other way for the expected form of attack from the rear. He gave it a quick burst and then pulled up a long, curving climb to join me. As he pulled alongside, he waved his arm down at the running German and nodded at me to get it. I went down on the Hun's tail and saw that Mick had killed the gunner, and I could attack safely. He had set the Hun up for me and deliberately killed the gunner to ensure that I got my kill.

His service with 40 Squadron ended on a high note. He believed in tactical flexibility and, wherever possible, in maximising the vital element of surprise. A surprised enemy, attacked from an unexpected direction will take seconds to react and evade. That's your window for killing him. The air fighting of 1918 was very much about attrition. His long-sightedness was legendary and a tremendous asset. He began the final year of the war serving in Britain where he met Ira Jones who came to revere him:

> The fact that I am still alive is due to Mick's high standard of leadership and the strict discipline on which he insisted. We were all expected to follow and cover him as far as possible during an engagement and then to rejoin the formation as soon as that engagement was over. None of Mick's pilots would have dreamed of chasing off alone after the retreating enemy or any other such foolhardy act. He moulded us into a team, and because of his skilled

leadership we became a highly efficient team. Our squadron leader said that Mannock was the most skilful patrol leader in World War I, which would account for the relatively few casualties in his flight team compared with the high number of enemy aircraft destroyed.

Like von Richthofen, Mannock was an inspirational teacher, though he had no love for the German ace: 'I hope he roasted the whole way down' was his only comment when the Red Baron finally cashed in. His gospel 'Gentlemen, always above, seldom on the same level; never underneath', spread, his individual preaching became the mantra of the RFC. He stressed the need for team work; air fighting was no longer for lone wolves. There were too many enemy formations in the sky, the wolf was dead meat.

Mannock scored over 60 kills and greatly influenced and inspired tactical innovation. On 26 July 1918 he took off on an induction flight to give newcomer Lieutenant Douglas Inglis, a Kiwi novice, his first taste of the Western Front and, hopefully, a taste of action. The action took the form of an LVG two-seater which was duly sent down in flames. Mannock, the master, then broke one of his own rules by diving to check the crash site. This was directly over enemy lines and his dive was greeted by a storm of ground fire. Generally, this wasn't effective but that day the infantry got lucky – bullets riddled his engine. Mannock crashed and was killed. He has no known grave. His testament survives:

1. Pilots must dive to attack with zest, and must hold their fire until they get within one hundred yards of the target.
2. Achieve surprise by approaching from the east (the German side of the front).
3. Utilize the sun's glare and clouds to achieve surprise.
4. Pilots must keep physically fit by exercise and the moderate use of stimulants.
5. Pilots must sight their guns and practice as much as possible. Targets are fleeting.
6. Pilots must practice spotting machines in the air and recognizing them at long range, and every aeroplane is to be treated as an enemy until it is certain it is not.

7. Pilots must learn where the enemy's blind spots are.

8. Scouts must attack from above and two-seaters from beneath their tails.

9. Pilots must practice quick turns, as this manoeuvre is used more than another in a fight.

10. Pilots must practice judging distances in flight as these are very deceptive.

11. Decoys must be guarded against – a single enemy is often a decoy – therefore the air above must be searched before attacking.

12. If the day is sunny, machines should be turned with as little bank as possible; otherwise the sun glistening on their wings will give away their positions at long range.

13. Pilots must keep turning in a dogfight and never fly straight unless firing.

14. Pilots must never dive away from an enemy, as he gives an opponent a non-deflection shot – bullets are faster than aeroplanes.

15. Pilots must keep an eye on their watches during patrols, on the direction and strength of the wind.

Perhaps the 'perfect' British ace was James McCudden. He was a middle-class lad who joined the Royal Engineers as a boy soldier, moving to the RFC as a mechanic in 1913. As a fitter he went to France with 3 Squadron, only getting into the air in 1915 as an observer. He survived the 'Fokker Scourge' then learned to fly, starting his fighter career with FE2bs and DH2s. He quickly notched up the five victories necessary to qualify for ace status. He was an astonishingly good pilot and Mannock was one of his

James Ira Thomas 'Taffy' Jones DSO MC DFC and Bar MM (1896–1960) flew as an observer before training as a pilot. He flew an SE5a and ended the war with 37 kills. He went on to serve in World War II, and was a friend and future biographer of Mannock.

students. Like Lanoe Hawker before him, he was a crack shot, the consummate professional. Partly this was down to natural aptitude but equally the fruit of much hard work, mastery of his weapons and assiduous practice. His guns were cleaned till they shone; rounds greased and carefully loaded to avoid stoppages. He was no dilettante.

After home service, he returned to the Front and began racking up kills. One of his most extraordinary adventures occurred late in 1916. On 27 December, he

James McCudden VC, 1917.

was on patrol over Arras and Monchy le Preux, soon to be the site of the bitterest fighting on the ground. His half-dozen DH2s scrapped with a bunch of Albatros fighters and McCudden swooped to the relief of one of his comrades. He plunged towards the DII but his gun jammed after barely 20 rounds. Soon an unkindness of black-crossed fighters was circling like vultures.

He dived to get clear but one came after him and it wasn't until he went into a spinning dive that the German pilot backed off. British Tommies on the ground were blasting at the Albatros. McCudden, his stoppage mercifully cleared, turned to give chase. When he got back to base, his mates were surprised, those who'd seen his spin though he was a goner and he'd already been posted as 'missing'. It is possible, though not confirmed, that this particular persistent Hun was none other than the Red Baron himself and McCudden had avoided being added to his score.

Aside from Ball, the British press had never lionised fighter aces in the manner of the French or Germans. That changed when Lord Northcliffe, an enthusiast for all things airborne and the influential proprietor of the *Daily Mail*, joined the Ministry of Information. On 3 January 1918 the paper ran a feature on 'Our Unknown Air Heroes'. This was McCudden's unexpected curtain call:

> What I want to know is why an Englishman whose hobby is bringing down sky Huns in braces and trios between luncheon and tea, who can already claim a bag of 30 enemy aircraft, should have to wait and be killed before a grateful nation waiting to acclaim him could even learn his name?
>
> I wonder if people in England realize that the German Air Service is the most popular and feted branch of the Kaiser's war machine because German authorities have imagination enough to exploit its personal side. How many people in these islands can name as many British airmen as there are fingers on one hand?

Like hyenas the rest of the press picked up the trend and McCudden found himself famous. He hated it, loathed publicity and was more concerned about how his fellow pilots would react. To him, like Mannock, the air war was corporate. Being an ace didn't matter.

On 9 July, still in England, McCudden called on his fiancée and handed her, among other things his medals (he was the highest decorated RFC pilot of the war). He'd also written a book and left the manuscript with her. He then flew over the Channel back to France but had to land to check directions – there was a heavy mist. He'd just taken off from the aerodrome at Auxi-le-Chateau when his plane crashed. It burst into flames but ground crew battled through to pull him clear. He lived for a few hours then died that evening.

With 26 victories, Eddie Rickenbacker was the Americans' highest scoring flyer. He was also a keen racing-car driver and designer. He survived the war and had a glittering career. The US press raised him to movie-star status until he was eclipsed by Lindbergh. He published a very lively memoir, *Fighting the Flying Circus*:

There was a scout coming towards us from north of Pont-à-Mousson. It was at about our altitude. I knew it was a Hun the moment I saw it, for it had the familiar lines of their new Pfalz. Moreover, my confidence in James Norman Hall was such that I knew he couldn't make a mistake. And he was still climbing into the sun, carefully keeping his position between its glare and the oncoming fighting plane I clung as closely to Hall as I could. The Hun was steadily approaching us, unconscious of his danger, for we were full in the sun.

With the first downward dive of Jimmy's machine I was by his side. We had at least a thousand feet advantage over the enemy and we were two to one numerically. He might out dive our machines, for the Pfalz is a famous diver, while our faster climbing Nieuports had a droll little habit of shedding their fabric when plunged too furiously through the air. The Boche hadn't a chance to out fly us. His only salvation would be in a dive towards his own lines.

These thoughts passed through my mind in a flash and I instantly determined upon my tactics. While Hall went in for his attack I would keep my altitude and get a position the other side of the Pfalz, to cut off his retreat.

No sooner had I altered my line of flight than the German pilot saw me leave the sun's rays. Hall was already half-way to him when he stuck up his nose and began furiously climbing to the upper ceiling. I let him pass me and found myself on the other side just as Hall began firing. I doubt if the Boche had seen Hall's Nieuport at all.

Surprised by discovering this new antagonist, Hall, ahead of him, the Pfalz immediately abandoned all idea of a battle and banking around to the right started for home, just as I had expected him to do. In a trice I was on his tail. Down, down we sped with throttles both full open. Hall was coming on somewhere in my rear. The Boche had no heart for evolutions or manoeuvres. He was running like a scared rabbit, as I had run from Campbell. I was gaining upon him every instant and had my sights trained dead upon his seat before I fired my first shot.

At 150 yards I pressed my triggers. The tracer bullets cut a streak of living fire into the rear of the Pfalz tail. Raising the nose of my aeroplane slightly the fiery streak lifted itself like the stream of water pouring from a garden hose. Gradually it settled into the pilot's seat. The swerving of the Pfalz course indicated that its rudder no longer was held by a directing hand. At 2000 feet above the enemy's lines I pulled up my headlong dive and watched the enemy machine continuing on its course. Curving slightly to the left the Pfalz circled a little to the south and the next minute crashed onto the ground just at the edge of the woods a mile inside their own lines. I had brought down my first enemy aeroplane and had not been subjected to a single shot!

William Barker was a Canadian infantryman who had transferred to the RFC from the infantry, one of those almost unimaginably courageous soldiers who'd stood firm against the German gas attack at the second battle of Ypres. He first flew as an observer but soon showed his hunter's credentials bringing down an Albatros on his fourth flight. He went on to train as a pilot and showed exceptional ability even with the ungainly RE8. Moving to the far more deadly Camel, he quickly racked up nine kills. He served both in the UK and on the Italian Front. By 1918 the Luftwaffe was heavily outnumbered but the sleek Fokker DVII was giving out a last hurrah. Barker transferred back to the Western Front, joining 201 Squadron, to fly the new Sopwith Snipe, the RAF's response to the DVII. By 26 October he had knocked down a hefty total of 46 enemy planes. He was, on that day, ordered home and set off next morning for the flight home. The trip should have been uneventful.

He had scarcely been in the air for 20 minutes before spotting a sedate Rumpler, temptingly close. Beware the lure of the easy victim as many aces had already found to their cost. He blitzed the lumbering two-seater which soon spiralled down to its death. He kept pace, making sure there'd be no second chances. But it wasn't just a bad day for the Germans he'd killed. Fire rippled through the air and a tracer round smashed the bone in his right leg. He couldn't get the damaged limb to respond so lost control of the right rudder. The pain was unimaginable.

As he banked he saw the scale of the opposition. He was flying into the maw of a full *jagdgeschwader*, four *jastas* in stepped formation. Three-score enemy now confronted him, all flying DVIIs. The situation calls to mind that of Grenville and the last fight of the *Revenge* – 'the one and the fifty-three'. Every schoolboy once knew how that ended. Despite his wound and despite the odds, he just charged, knocking down the plane that had first fired on him.

One down and only 59 to go! He swiftly made that just 58, his second victim exploding in flames. His adversaries, confident his lone plane wasn't the tip of an unpleasant iceberg, gave him their full and undivided attention, bouncing his aircraft in packs of five with more in reserve above and below. Whatever manoeuvre he attempted, he'd be open to attack. Three hundred bullets riddled the Snipe and he was hit again, this time in the left leg. He could barely operate the rudder at all and was flying by joystick and throttle.

The cockpit was awash with his blood and he temporarily passed out. The plane went into a spin but, providentially, the rush of air brought him round. He'd dropped 6,000 feet and the hungry bees were still on his shot-up tail. Despite the pain and blood loss he was still full of fight and determined he'd ram whichever German got nearest. He still had ammunition and scored another DVII before he received his third wound as a round hit his left elbow. He passed out again and the aircraft went into another spin. Somehow he came round again and got the Snipe into a straight line again. He could now only use one of his four limbs. Being so low discouraged his pursuers and, in his lucid moments he was able to think about how and where he might land.

Where was a handy field, just behind the British lines? How was pretty rough. He skidded down at 90 mph, sheered the wheels and numerous other parts, bounced a few times and ended up with the shattered undercarriage in the air. The Scots from the Highland Light Infantry who pulled him free assumed from his shop-worn state and the amount of blood decorating the wrecked cockpit that they were dragging out a corpse. They weren't. Though in a coma for ten days, he made a full recovery and was given his Victoria Cross by King George V in person. He'd brought down four enemy aircraft in forty minutes and survived the most unequal aerial duel of the entire war. A dozen days later and it was finally over.

The war in the air was not glamorous, no war ever is. It was not chivalric or poetic. It was hard, bloody, brutal, lonely, and infinitely perilous. The rate of attrition was fierce and relentless. Nonetheless these flyers, these superlative aces, were heroes in the true sense. There was honour in their quest, and steadfastness, loyalty and, above all, a sublime courage. In the words of the benediction, we should remember them.

Flying alone! Nothing gives such a sense of mastery over mechanism, mastery indeed over space, time and life itself, as this. A hundred miles, north, south, east, west, thirty thousand square miles of unbroken cloud plains! No traveller in the desert, no pioneer to the Poles had ever seen such an expanse of sand or snow. Only the lonely threshers of the sky, hidden from the earth, had gazed on it. Only we who went up into the high places in the shadow of wings!

Cecil Lewis

CHAPTER 3

THEIR FINEST HOUR

1939–41

*This man had kept a school
And rode our wingèd horse;
This other his helper and friend
Was coming into his force;
He might have won fame in the end,
So sensitive his nature seemed,
So daring and sweet his thought.
This other man I had dreamed
A drunken, vainglorious lout.
He had done most bitter wrong
To some who are near my heart,
Yet I number him in the song;
He, too, has resigned his part
In the casual comedy;
He, too, has been changed in his turn,
Transformed utterly:
A terrible beauty is born.*

W. B. Yeats, *Easter 1916*

IN THE CENTURY-LONG HISTORY OF FIGHTER AIRCRAFT, none is more celebrated than the Supermarine Spitfire, perhaps the most famous plane that has ever flown. That summer of 1940 is perhaps the most defining of all aerial conflicts – the Battle of Britain, as totemic and potent as any Arthurian battle. As

Winston Churchill told the House of Commons on 18 June 1940:

> What General Weygand has called The Battle of France is over. The battle of Britain is about to begin. Upon this battle depends the survival of Christian civilisation. Upon it depends our own British life and the long continuity of our institutions and our Empire. The whole fury and might of the enemy must very soon be turned on us. . . . Let us therefore brace ourselves to our duties, and so bear ourselves that, if the British Empire and its Commonwealth last for a thousand years, men will still say, 'This was their finest hour'.

Those few

As an aircraft builder working for Supermarine Aviation in the early 1930s, R. J. Mitchell (1895–1937) became aware of how German aircraft design, particularly of single-seat fighters, was racing ahead of British efforts. The mainstay of the RAF was the Hawker Hurricane, a handy plane and a stable gun platform, easy to fly but outmatched by the advanced 'monocoque' design of the Me 109. The idea of monocoque construction came from Eugene Ruchonnet. Rather than mounting panels, a monocoque

The **Hawker Hurricane** was the workhorse of the RAF in 1940. It had been introduced three years earlier but its box girder primary fuselage structure was already out of date. It was slower than the Me 109 but handier and more agile. Despite being outclassed it would still account for some 60 per cent of the RAF's total kills during the Battle of Britain. It served throughout the war – over 14,500 were built.

airplane's skin supports much of the load, with some internal bracing and bulkheads in place to maintain structural integrity. Mitchell was already in poor health, and he had been warned that over-work would kill him. He chose to sacrifice himself. Day and night, he worked to leave the RAF and Britain, for that matter the free world, his brilliant legacy. He died before the war but lived long enough to see his design the Supermarine Spitfire fly.

The Luftwaffe had experimented on Guernica during the course of the Spanish Civil War. Both Herman Göring and Arthur 'Bomber' Harris drew the wrong conclusions: that strategic air power alone could bring an enemy to his knees. Göring's other mistake was the overall concept of the Luftwaffe. It was a superb *tactical* air force but unsuited to a *strategic* role. The Battle of Britain itself was one of attrition; whoever's nerve broke first would lose. It was a close-run thing, ending in stalemate with both sides fought out. Losses in terms of numbers were almost even but any German shot down over England would be captured whilst RAF crew, if they lived and were whole, might fly again.

Having won the Battle of France, the Luftwaffe re-grouped into three *luftflotten* (air fleets). Luftflotte 2, commanded by Generalfeldmarschall Albert Kesselring ('Smiling Albert'), was

The **Messerschmitt Bf 109** (commonly known as the **Me 109**) was the backbone of German fighter command at the start of the war. a superb all-metal monocoque design – a world-class plane. Synchronised machine guns were fitted to the fuselage to keep the wing structure light and, latterly a 20 mm cannon was fitted to fire through the propeller shaft.

to be responsible for the bombing of south-east England and the London area. Luftflotte 3, under Generalfeldmarschall Hugo Sperrle, targeted the West Country, Wales, the Midlands, and north-west England. Luftflotte 5, led by Generaloberst Hans-Jürgen Stumpff from his lair in Norway, looked towards the north of England and Scotland. As the fighting raged, command responsibility shifted, with Luftflotte 3 taking more responsibility for the night-time Blitz attacks while the main daylight operations fell to Luftflotte 2.

Early German predictions suggested it would take a mere four days to blitz RAF Fighter Command in southern England. This would be followed by a further four-week offensive during which twin-engined bombers and long-range fighters would destroy all military installations throughout the country and smash British capacity to produce more planes. The campaign would commence with attacks on aerodromes near the beaches, gradually creeping inland to deplete that magic circle of sector airfields protecting the capital.

Subsequent adjustments gave the Luftwaffe five weeks, running from 8 August to 15 September, to win hegemony over English skies. To achieve this objective, which would signal an effective end to the war, Fighter Command had to be wasted, either on the ground or in the air. In achieving this, the Luftwaffe needed a clear win; not a draw or a pyrrhic victory that would leave it too weak to support any subsequent amphibious invasion. There was only one alternative strategy: to repeat Guernica on a far larger scale, devastating British cities. For the moment, Hitler baulked at this.

Overall, the Battle of Britain can be divided into four pretty distinct phases: 10 July–11 August, *Kanalkampf* ('the Channel battles'); 12–23 August, *Adlerangriff* ('Eagle Attack'), the grandly dubbed onslaught against the coastal airfields; 24 August–6 September, drenching the aerodromes generally. Finally, and most critically; 7 September onwards, the raids switched to targeting towns and cities.

One of those 'up' on 10 July was Ira Jones, hero of the previous war with 40 kills. At this point the Welshman was a rear-echelon wing commander based at a training field. Some 63 Ju 88s were approaching the West Country – radar warning came too late to scramble fighters. 'Grandpa Tiger' Jones was not one to be deterred by the odds or the fact his antiquated Henley target-tug was totally unarmed. He had knocked down plenty of Germans in the last show and wasn't about to let a fresh opportunity pass.

Jones got onto the tail of one Ju 88 – 'I felt the old joy of action coursing through my body.' His only weapon was a Very pistol which fired a pretty multi-coloured cartridge. He came in front of the German pilot, banked and fired off his single flare. The bomber was lit up like a Christmas tree. It worked, the German promptly sheered off and ran for it.

The **Messerschmitt Bf 110** (or *Jabo* as it was nicknamed) was a heavy twin-engined fighter introduced in 1937. It was an impressive gun bus sporting two 20 mm cannon and four 7.92 mm machine guns. Its abiding weakness was a lack of agility.

In the air the Luftwaffe preferred to fly in a loose section of two (nicknamed the *rotte*); a leader (*rottenführer*), followed at say 200 metres by his wingman (*rottenhund* or *katschmarkes*), who also flew slightly higher and was trained to stay with his boss. Two of these pairs formed a four-man flight (*schwarm*). Each flight in the squadron (*staffel*) flew at staggered heights around 200 metres apart, making the whole formation trickier to spot at a distance and facilitating flexibility. By using a tight cross-over turn, the *schwarm* could quickly change direction. Slower and heavier Bf 110s adopted similar tactics.

The RAF during the inter-war years had planned to meet enemy bomber offensives, fighters had been ruled out. So the tactical imperative had been the ability to concentrate and deliver a hefty punch. These 'fighting area tactics' focused on a series of flying manoeuvres aimed at maximizing firepower. Fighters were expected to fly in tight, v-shaped flights ('vics') of three, with four vics in tight formation. By 1940 this was outmoded and the Luftwaffe's more flexible approach clearly superior.

Well-armed but lacking agility, Bf 110s proved vulnerable to nimbler RAF fighters. This meant the bulk of bomber nannies would have to be made up of Me 109s. Though the need to protect vulnerable bombers was paramount, Göring, who knew all about aces' hunting instincts, was keen to free up fighters for 'free hunts' (*freie jagd*). Fleet-winged Me 109s would range ahead of the bombers like beaters flushing game. The closer the fighters were tied to the bombers' apron strings the harder it was for them to maneouvre and losses in dogfights climbed accordingly.

RAF fighter controllers with their finely tuned antennae, latterly in the Filter rooms, were often able to detect these skirmishers and move squadrons around to avoid them. Dowding's plan was always to conserve his fighters in order to inflict maximum damage on German bombers. Extending their hunters' lures, the Luftwaffe resorted to adding small formations of bombers as tastier bait, covering them with packs of Me 109s.

We have the classic image of RAF flyers, chilling in deck chairs, fully kitted and tense for the call while the cloudless blue sky of a quintessential English summer begins to vibrate with the thrumming of bomber engines. At the age of 21, Pilot Officer John Beard flew his Hurricane in defence of London. One cloudless summer afternoon, Beard's squadron was scrambled, racing to their planes, deafened by the roar of propellers as they climbed to 15,000 feet:

> Minutes went by. Green fields and roads were now beneath us. I scanned the sky and the horizon for the first glimpse of the Germans. A new vector came through on the R.T. [radio telephone] and we swung round with the sun behind us. Swift on the heels of this I heard Yellow flight leader call through the earphones. I looked quickly toward Yellow's position, and there they were!
>
> It was really a terrific sight and quite beautiful. First they seemed just a cloud of light as the sun caught the many glistening chromium parts of their engines, their windshields, and the spin of their airscrew discs. Then, as our squadron hurtled nearer, the details stood out. I could see the bright-yellow noses of Messerschmitt fighters sandwiching the bombers, and could even pick out some of the types. The sky seemed full of them, packed in layers thousands of feet deep. They came on steadily, wavering up and down along the horizon. 'Oh, golly,' I thought, 'golly, golly…'

Orders came through the earphones and the Hurricanes circled to begin their attack, screaming down like maniacal banshees. Beard kept both hands on the stick, 'You have to steady a fighter just as you have to steady a rifle before you fire it.' The afternoon sky was full of aircraft, a maelstrom of planes. Beard focused on his target, a Heinkel, swelling in his vision till it locked in the red dot of his sights. He wondered why the bomber didn't move, then his finger clenched the trigger. Eight Brownings hammered away, two bursts each of as many seconds, acrid stench of cordite filling the cockpit.

His rush took him above the quarry. He saw rounds hitting, a red glow blossoming inside the canopy, bursting out into streaks of flame. The bomber staggered and began its final fall, detritus spinning off. There were more. He climbed and saw another flock of bombers circled by shepherding Me 109s. As he raced in he detected three fast flights of Spitfires coming up, breaking into a fleur-de-lys attack, carving a bloody swathe through the invaders. Eight of the enemy went down.

The sprawling melée had spread out over London. He could see the streets and parks below, laid out like a familiar jigsaw, 'I had an instant's glimpse of the Round Pond, where I sailed boats as a child.' This was a rather different game. He spotted a Dornier hotly chased by a Hurricane. A British fighter in turn, stalked by two Me 109s. The Hurricane pilot hadn't seen them but neither had they spotted Beard. He charged head on, into the teeth of one, shooting him literally to pieces. He aimed at the other but the German executed a smart Immelmann half-turn and got clear. Beard had no time to celebrate as another brace were now on his tail. He managed a fairly smart climb himself, tracer streaking underneath. He was low on fuel and ammo, happily so were they and broke off.

As the first stage of the battle ground on, Flight Lieutenant Dennis Robinson was in the air on 8 August. Flying his Spitfire he had nailed two Me 109s during July. This wasn't going to be one of his better days. He and his wingman had already seen action, chasing bombers and firing off all their rounds (eight

The **Chain Home** system comprised a ring of coastal Early Warning stations – all called 'radar' in 1940. Chain Home was the first operational early warning radar system in the world. The 'Dowding' System was another first – named after its creator; a wide area ground-controlled interception network, spread over the whole of Britain.

machine guns eat up ammo at a prodigious rate and will run out after 15 seconds shooting). Robinson was flying in the prescribed tight vic formation, his and the wingman's eyes playing 'follow my leader' as instructed. They'd not spotted a stalking party of Messerschmitts coming up from behind.

'The first thing I felt was the thud of bullets hitting my aircraft and a long line of tracer bullets streaming out ahead of my Spitfire. In a reflex action I slammed the stick forward as far as it would go…' The Spitfire stood on its head, propeller pointing downwards. Fear kicked in; that brief euphoria gone. His plane rocketed earthwards. He strained to pull back and level off, start looking for his enemy. Smoke was beginning to billow from the engine. He had a terror of burning to death. There was no fire, rounds had pierced and emptied the glycol tank. The motor stalled. By some mysterious alchemy the skies had emptied.

Should he bail out or not? It was always risky and he feared the dying plane might yet kill civilians on crashing. He decided to attempt a belly-flop landing in what looked like a suitable field. So far so good. The Spitfire slid over damp grass then abruptly did a 360 degree roll and slammed down on her back, jamming the canopy. The plane finally ended up nose down, tail in the air stuck in a hidden ditch. Bad as this could potentially be, Robinson was able to get the canopy back, finally clear his harness and walk away from the wreck. He flew again next day.

By September, as both sides remained locked like punch-drunk fighters, tactics had fused. A *freie jagd* would sweep in ahead of the main bomber formations, flying in at altitudes of 16,000–20,000 feet, closely shepherded by fighters. Escorts were divided into two wings (*gruppen*), some maintaining close liaison with the bombers, keeping more a few hundred yards distant and maintaining height. If the formation was attacked from starboard, that flank engaged the attackers, the high cover moving to starboard and the port wing shifting upwards.

When the threat emerged from port the previous drill was reversed. British fighters coming from behind were met by the back markers and the two flanking wings dropped to the rear. If the threat came from above, the top group responded while the flanks sought height to chase RAF fighters down as they broke contact. If attacked from all sides, the whole lot flew in defensive circles. By late summer, the Luftwaffe had had plenty scope to hone its hybrid tactics. But they still weren't winning. Me 109 pilots were severely hamstrung by the lack of long-range fuel tanks (only partially introduced towards the end of the battle). German fighters had just over an hour in the air. Once over Britain, a Messerschmitt pilot had to keep an eye on the red warning light. Once this flashed, he was forced to head back. And back meant flying over the Channel. Pilots generally don't like water, fearful of *Kanalkrankheit* ('Channel sickness').

James Harry 'Ginger' Lacey was a Yorkshire lad, educated at King James Grammar School in Knaresborough and then at Leeds Technical College. He studied pharmacy but also joined the RAF Volunteer Reserve. Trained at Perth before qualifying as

Air Chief Marshal Hugh Dowding (1882–1970) was a career RAF commander who had served with fighters on the Western Front during World War I. Between the wars he was responsible for UK air defence and as Commander-in-Chief Fighter Command, he led the RAF during the crucial weeks of the Battle of Britain. He is rightly credited as the architect of victory. A reserved and aloof character, nicknamed 'Stuffy' on account of his perceived humourlessness, he lacked the tact and finesse to survive service politics and rivalries. He was eventually replaced by Sholto Douglas, an advocate of 'big wing' as opposed to more Fabian tactics.

an instructor back in Yorkshire, he had amassed over a thousand hours flying time before being called up in 1939 and posted to 501 Squadron.

He was blooded in the Battle for France. During the course of that fateful, disastrous May, he downed a Heinkel, an Me 109 and Bf 1110 in one single day. Before the month was out and the battle lost, he'd bagged two more bombers. He didn't get out completely unscathed. On 9 June he was forced down, smacking into wet ground and was lucky to avoid drowning. His exploits earned him a Croix de Guerre from the host nation.

During the Battle of Britain, 501 Squadron was stationed either at Gravesend or Croydon in the very thick of the fight. On 20 July Lacey claimed the first of many victories, destroying an Me 109. During early August he scored a string of hits and 'probables', a brace of Stukas, several Dorniers, Me 109s and Bf 110s. Fire from an intended victim, a Heinkel this time, shot up his plane on 13 August and he had to bale out. Again, he was unwounded and on the 23rd he was awarded the Distinguished Flying Medal (DFM).

As August came to a thundering close, he riddled two more enemy aircraft – shooting down an He 111 and shooting up another Bf 110. He took more than a few hits in the fight. Over the Thames Estuary, and perhaps mindful of his previous experience, he decided to avoid the 'drink', he managed to glide the plane back and land safely. September brought plenty of fresh trade. By the end of the first week he'd downed four more Messerschmitts and damaged a Dornier. Friday 13 September was surely unlucky for the Luftwaffe: that day he bagged one of those impudent He 111s which had just bombed the king's residence at Buckingham Palace. The fight ended with another parachute drop. His luck held and he sustained only minor injuries.

Ginger Lacey, like most British and Allied pilots, was only too well aware of the limitations of RAF doctrine. Flyers began to adopt more flexible tactics with skirmishers or 'weavers' flying above and behind. It was a good idea but these were apt to become the first casualties in a scrap. Adolph 'Sailor' Malan, leading 74 Squadron, stole a leaf from the enemy's book adopting the 'fours in line astern' formation. Malan's innovation soon became the general norm.

During 15 September, a day of particularly savage fighting, now commemorated as 'Battle of Britain Day', 'Ginger' got another He 111 and three Messerschmitts. Later he bounced a full dozen Me 109s and shot down two more. A mere two days later he was obliged to jump for it yet again. By the end of the battle he would have either bailed out or crash landed no fewer than nine times! As autumn drew on and into drear November, he racked up 23 kills and added a bar to his DFM. He continued to serve throughout the war and then, in peacetime, ran a successful air freight business. Ginger Lacey died in 1989.

Martin Pinfold commanded 56 Squadron at North Weald. By late August they had been fully in the brunt of it and taken quite heavy casualties, including two of his flight commanders. In his first five days, he was scrambled over a dozen times. New pilots were coming in from those who'd served in Czech and Polish air forces. These flyers had, in many instances, flown against the Luftwaffe in defence of their homelands. They had scores to settle and their contribution to the battle would be immense.

On 30 September the squadron went aloft to take on German raiders over Portland. Their target was an aircraft manufacturing complex at Yeovil. Pinfold could muster no more than half a dozen Hurricanes for the fight. The bombers were well guarded and he decided on a flanking approach to give his squadron the best chance of knocking down a few:

Within seconds I was caught up in a frantic dog fight. I shot down one DO 215 but was hit by return fire. The cooling tank in my Hurricane exploded and the cockpit filled with fumes. I could hardly see a thing but I managed to nurse the plane down safely. We later discovered the bombing raid had been a disaster. Because of the thick cloud the Germans had dropped their bombs by mistake on Sherborne causing huge loss of civilian life. It became known as Black Monday.

One of those Czech pilots with scores to settle was Josef František. Born in 1914, before his nation came into existence, he joined their air force in 1934. As the jackboot stamped down on his country, he escaped to Poland. He fought against the Germans there in 1939, and was shot down. With what remained of his unit, he made it out to Romania. He was interned but soon removed himself to France where he joined the Free Poles. When his host nation fell, he again escaped, this time to Britain where he joined 303 Squadron, made up mainly of Poles. On 2 September, he bagged his first Me 109.

If he was brilliant, he was also idiosyncratic, a throwback to the maverick aces of the Great War. He disdained formation flying and expected everyone else to get out of his way. Like Albert Ball, he became a lone hunter, a law unto himself. He was very good at killing Germans. Kent was his favourite stalking ground, bouncing enemy fighters as they returned over the Channel. He scored 17 kills that month, mostly Messerschmitts. He became a top Battle of Britain ace and on 30 September, was awarded the Distinguished Flying Cross (DFC). Barely a week later he was killed when he crashed on landing. Some said he was trying to impress his girlfriend with some fancy flying. Without him, and those other very brave young men from Poland and Czechoslovakia, the battle might not have been won.

On the other side flew Bader's unlikely friend Adolf 'Dolfo' Galland. Almost an old man by fighter pilot standards, Galland had trained on gliders in 1929, becoming a civilian flyer three years later. He first joined the armed forces of the doomed Weimar Republic, transferring to the Luftwaffe in 1934. He gained his combat wings with the Condor Legion fighting the proxy war in Spain. His specialty was ground attack; he wrote manuals on the subject. The invasion of Poland saw him in action again. It wasn't till 1940 and the Battle for France that he transferred to fighters. It was a good choice from Göring's perspective. By the end of the year Galland had notched up 57 kills. Come the close of the following year, he'd boosted that to

96, surpassing von Richthofen. Later in the war, on the death of his predecessor, he assumed command of the overall fighter arm and retired from combat missions. His final tally stood at 104. Adolf Galland survived the war and died in 1996.

During the battle, the brunt of the fighting fell on Air Vice Marshal Keith Park's 11 Group, tasked with the defence of London and the south-east. Park was a canny tactician who toured his airfields in a personalised Hurricane. An advocate of Dowding's defensive approach, he sent up individual squadrons rather than larger numbers. He was able to cope with the Luftwaffe but not with Air Vice Marshal Trafford Leigh Mallory, commanding 12 Group, responsible for the Midlands and East Anglia. Leigh Mallory was ambitious and irked by his secondary role. His theory of how to deal with the Germans was more aggressive, based on the 'big wing' or 'Balbo' solution. He would put up three to five squadrons to take the enemy head on, rather the kind of battle Göring had been hoping for. Douglas Bader

Group Captain Sir Douglas Bader (1910–82) joined the RAF in 1928. Two years later, in a flying accident, he lost both legs. Famously, he refused to let this stop him and flew with prosthetics. He scored first while covering the retreat to Dunkirk and went on to win 22 victories confirmed with as many 'probables' or part-kills. A great supporter of Trafford Leigh Mallory and the 'big wing' theory, he was captured after having to bail out over France a year later. Despite his disability, his penchant for escaping landed him in Colditz though not before he had stuck up an unlikely friendship with top German ace Adolf Galland.

Erick Lock, July/August 1941.

was his exceptionally bullish subordinate. Both proved adept at high-level intrigue, finally engineering both Park's and Dowding's sideways shifts. The effects of the Blitz didn't help. Nonetheless, history would vindicate Dowding, and Park went on to conduct the desperate glory of the air defence of Malta in 1942.

Top RAF scorer during the Battle was Eric Stanley Lock, born in 1919 of farming stock on the Welsh Marches. Had there been no war, he might have stayed a farmer. His love of vehicles and things mechanical took him into the RAVR in February 1939. On 31 August his reserve outfit was disbanded and the pilots called up. By the end of October he was training for war in the air. He earned his wings in March 1940 but didn't fly a Spitfire till two months after and first took off in anger only that August.

Stationed at Catterick, he was denied any real action until 15 August when the Germans sought to test the RAF's resilience by attacking both north and south. Just north of the town Lock fell upon a mixed force of Ju 88s and their Bf 110 escorts. He pounced on one of the heavy fighters; setting both engines on fire and then accounted for one of the bombers. On 3 September, the first anniversary of the war, 41 Squadron was moved to Hornchurch. There was no shortage of trade over the Thames Estuary.

Two days later, he flew as his squadron leader's wingman when the new arrivals took on a flock of Heinkels and their Me 109 escorts. He clobbered two of the bombers but made the cardinal mistake of following his second kill too far down. A Messerschmitt was swiftly on his tail, fast as a scorpion, guns rattling. Lock took damage to his Spitfire and a wound to the leg. Undeterred, he yanked back into a savage climb, surprising the German who stalled as he sped after. Roles reversed, Lock stalked his enemy's dive and shot him to pieces. Meanwhile his second Heinkel had ditched in the sea. From the air he guided a boat to pick up survivors. He got another Me 109 that same day.

Despite his wound – and against doctor's advice – he was back in the air next morning. The injury didn't seem to cramp his style. He brought down a Ju 88 off Dover. On 9 September he racked up another pair and two more on the 11th. He now had nine victories and very soon a DFC. On 20 September, he jumped a trio of He 111s and destroyed one. The other two bolted. During that same sortie he spotted a Henschel Hs 126 which he chased clear across the blue sea, downing it over the muzzles of German shore batteries at Boulogne. He'd won 15 victories in just 16 days and added a bar to his DFC.

After R&R, it was back to Hornchurch early in October. Lock was soon back out hunting and got another Me 109 on the 5th (with two 'probables'); on the 9th another definite and one 'probable'. More kills followed and before the end of the month he'd raised his score to 21. On 8 November, he had a near-miss when he had to ditch in a field in East Sussex. Luckily, he walked away.

On 17 November his squadron took on a swarm of Messerschmitts riding shotgun for bombers over the capital. He nailed one and damaged another when his own plane was shot up by cannon fire. He was hit in the right arm and both legs. By a bizarre stroke of luck, one of the rounds cut off the control lever and left the throttle at maximum. The crippled Spitfire shot off like a hare, escaping its pursuers; probably what Lock would have attempted had he not been too injured to try! This was just a reprieve. He was too shot up to bail out and couldn't slow down. He got below 2,000 feet, cut the engine and glided over RAF Martlesham Heath. Somehow he brought the aircraft down in one piece, though he was stuck in the wreck for two very long hours.

The squaddies who found him had to improvise a stretcher using rifles as poles and greatcoats for the sling. By the time they carried him two miles he had passed out from loss of blood, not helped by being dropped three times. Recovery required 15 operations and months of convalescence. Along with Richard Hilary he spent time in the Royal Masonic Hospital, operated on by the brilliant Sir Archibald McIndoe.

Despite his injuries, Lock returned to active service, back with 41 Squadron. By now, in the summer of 1941, the air battle was being fought over France. In July he downed another three Me 109s, showing he'd not lost his magic touch. On 3 August, returning from a sortie he spotted the very tempting target of an Axis column near Pas de Calais. He dived into a strafing run and was never seen again, simply vanished, presumably a victim of intensive ground fire. No trace of him or his Spitfire was ever found or recorded.

Above Mediterranean Shores

The Desert Air Force (DAF) variously known as Air HQ Western Desert, the Western Desert Air Force and First Tactical Air Force, performed a vital role during the North African War. Formed in 1941 to provide close air support to the British

Eighth Army, DAF comprised squadrons drawn from the Royal Air Force, its South African and Australian counterparts and latterly the USAAF. Prior to the formation of a united air arm, RAF Middle East Command, then under Air Chief Marshal Sir William Mitchell, was responsible for a quartet of different regions; Egypt, Malta, Iraq and Aden. When war broke out in the Mediterranean theatre the RAF, now under Air Vice-Marshal Sir Arthur Longmore, had some 29 squadrons with no more than 300 machines spread over this vast canvas.

In Egypt, Air Commodore Raymond Collishaw could deploy nine squadrons and the primary tasks revolved mostly around support and aerial reconnaissance with the odd dogfight against planes of Mussolini's Regia Aeronautica. Three squadrons were equipped with Gladiators, largely outdated, one with Lysanders and several squadrons of medium bombers, Blenheims and Bombays. Despite the disparity in numbers the RAF, soon augmented by Hawker Hurricanes, began to gain ascendancy through aggressive tactics and a certain sleight of hand. They successfully managed to convince the Italians they were facing rather more squadrons than was the case.

At the end of July 1941 Collishaw handed over to Air Vice-Marshal Coningham. By the end of the year, the whole of Middle East Air Command came under the aegis of Air Marshal Arthur Tedder, destined to be one of Montgomery's most bitter opponents. Three wings were deployed in the skies over North Africa: 258 and 269 Wings covered the front with 262 Wing held in reserve over the Nile Delta. As the direct threat to the homeland receded, more and newer machines were sent to the Mediterranean, mostly Hurricanes and the Douglas Boston medium bomber.

During the blistering North African summer of 1941, Australian Air Force pilot Clive Caldwell was flying a P-40. The Americans named this the Kittyhawk but Allied air forces designated it as the Tomahawk, a rather more aggressive designation. To emphasise the fact, desert flyers painted a symbolic shark's mouth on the nose. Although inferior to the Me 109 or Focke-Wulf 190, the Tomahawk did good service. 'Killer' Caldwell would become a top scorer.

By August, the Aussie had completed 40 missions and had scored a single Me 109. As he skimmed above the blistering sand below, he watched his plane's shadow. He loosed off a burst, noting the pattern of strikes relative to the aircraft. This was an epiphany moment, he realised he could work out the deflection needed to hit a moving target. He refined his method and within weeks had accounted for a quartet of enemy. His 'shadow-shooting' became the grail of gunnery drill. Just as well, on 29 August he was bounced by a brace of Messerschmitts. One was piloted by the von Richthofen of the sands, Leutnant Werner Schröer who had racked up an astonishing 114 kills.

Caldwell was in line to become number 115. At the first pass the German pair shot a hundred rounds of machine-gun fire through the Tomahawk, together with a handspan of 20 mm cannon shells. Caldwell suffered multiple wounds. Next time round more hits smashed the canopy, near blinding him whilst two more exploding shells blasted through the fuselage behind

The **Gloster Gladiator** or Gloster SS.37 was the RAF's last serving biplane, introduced early in 1937. Despite being outmoded, the plane did good service and was still in use with some air forces in the 1950s. The leading Gladiator ace was South African Marmaduke 'Pat' Pattle, who knocked down 15 enemy planes in a Gladiator. His final score all round was much higher before his Hurricane crashed during a dogfight over Greece in April 1941.

the pilot's seat and splintered the starboard wing. Caldwell was by now really annoyed; *quite hostile* in fact. He turned his ravaged plane into the attack and, against the odds, brought down the German ace's wingman. Schröer, his Me 109 also shot up, decided the Australian was the one that got away and fled. This wasn't much consolation as the Tomahawk was now on fire. Caldwell executed a sudden slip which succeeded in scotching the flames and somehow nursed the stricken aircraft safely home.

Throughout 1942, DAF provided long-range interdiction and tactical support to Eighth Army though its fighters were significantly outclassed by the German Messerschmitt 109 E and F variants which inflicted heavy losses. It was not until August, with the arrival of Spitfires, that the strategic balance in air-to-air combat shifted in the Allies' favour. In part, this was due to a shift in tactical doctrines, utilising the Luftwaffe concept of close army cooperation through the deployment of forward air controllers (the DAF's answer to the gunners' Forward Observers). DAF then began to deploy 'cab-ranks' of fighter-bombers, waiting to be directed onto specific targets. The tactic gave DAF control of the desert skies and provided significant and highly effective tactical support to Eighth Army during Second Alamein, the pursuit and Tunisian campaign.

Werner Schröer (1918–85) joined the Luftwaffe in 1937, initially as ground crew. He served through most of the North African campaign before being assigned to homeland defence. He rose steadily as his kills grew, being awarded the Knight's Cross of the Iron Cross with Oak Leaves and Swords. He survived the war and died aged 66 in 1985.

The DAF contained many pilots from German-occupied territories; 112 Squadron mainly comprised Polish airmen. The Polish Fighting Team ('Skalski's Circus') was attached to 145 Squadron. Unquestionably the most famous and successful Axis air formation engaged in the Desert War was Jagdgeschwader 27 'Afrika'. I Gruppe was first deployed to support Rommel in the Gazala battle in April 1961, led by Hauptmann 'Edu' Neumann. On 19 April, JG27 claimed its first four combat 'kills', more would soon follow. German fighter formations, prizing the 'Red Baron' spirit of competitive aces, flew their superior Me 109Es ('Emils') and latterly the F or 'Friedrich' types with great skill, technically and often qualitatively superior. II Gruppe arrived in theatre in September and then III Gruppe was sent from the Eastern Front in November.

The Great Siege

Malta is a discarded jewel in the Mediterranean, chucked halfway between Europe and Africa. It has suffered hostile intentions from both continents for centuries. In 1565, it was the final bastion of the Knights of St John in their long crusade against Islam. All-conquering Suleiman the Magnificent (who had driven the Hospitallers from their previous refuge on Rhodes over forty years before) decided to finish the job and sent a vast army to see to it. They failed and the knights, at considerable cost, held on. The Turks were decimated.

In May 1941, Rommel had similar leanings; he could see how vital possession of the island was to hegemony over the Mediterranean. The Axis had been bombing Malta since June 1940 but as the desert pendulum began its numerous swings, the intensity of raids increased exponentially. The Italians and Germans would, combined, fly over 3,000 sorties until November 1942. Montgomery's victory over the Germans and Italians at El Alamein signalled the beginning of the end (or end of the beginning as Churchill preferred). The RAF lost over 400 aircraft and 2,300 personnel, the Axis rather more. The Royal Navy lost heavily too – including two carriers. Nonetheless Malta accounted for 2,300 enemy ships and over 17,000 of their crews. Though the barb in the Axis hide was never quite prised free, Malta was virtually flattened and 1,500 civilians died. It was a desperate fight.

Nobody would have prophesied that Adrian Warburton would have become either an ace or one of the heroes of the hour. In fact, most would have been surprised he'd ever been given charge of a plane. His father had served on submarines and been based on Malta in the previous war. 'Warby' had gone to St Edward's School in England, which could number amongst its alumni both Douglas Bader and Guy Gibson. That's impressive but people weren't too impressed with Warby. They found him eccentric, aloof, a maverick loner whose only interests at school (by his own account) were masturbation and aviation. He would come to excel in at least one of these.

His parents were not too keen on the idea of him joining the RAF and he didn't enlist till 1938, by which time he was 20. The RAF turned out to be none too keen either. They could discern no germ of brilliance; his take-offs and landings frightened everyone, especially those in the aircraft with him. A series of desultory postings followed, passed to and fro like a poisoned chalice and frequently sent on a variety of courses to get him out of everyone's way. A disastrous marriage and mounting debts didn't help, his career hung by a thread.

He flew to Malta during late 1940 as the Axis ring began to bite. He was part of a much-needed photo reconnaissance unit, three crews in outmoded light attack bombers, Glenn Martin Marylands. Navigation and photography turned out to be his natural elements. He excelled at both, aided by exceptional eyesight and spatial awareness plus an apparent total lack of fear. Nobody trusted him to actually fly the plane but, when a couple of pilots went down with 'Malta Dog', his commanding officer had little choice. Getting the plane into the air and back down again in one piece still proved challenging but once in the air he had no equal, a virtuoso, a concert pianist amongst piano players. Warby had arrived.

As a photo reconnaissance ('PR') pilot his job was intelligence and he was very good at it. His work as the eyes of Malta made a palpable difference, especially as the Royal Navy was about to square up to Il Duce's proud navy at anchor in Taranto. The one thing a PR pilot was not supposed to do was engage in dog-fighting but Warby was a law unto himself. On 10 October he flew a pretty hairy mission over Taranto which was bristling with anti-aircraft (AA) batteries. Masked by dense low cloud, he got in and out again while still finding time to engage and shoot down an Italian seaplane, his first kill.

Continuing bad weather did not slow him down. He flew when other pilots wouldn't. The Italians shared the latter view which provided Warby with an element of surprise. On his next sortie he flew at mast height over the massed fleet before the AA gunners realised there was anyone daft enough to be up there. The Maryland, with the wind howling through the many bullet holes in her ageing hull, got clear. But Warby found the count of battleships didn't tally so he swung round and went back in again. This time the gunners were very much awake but still he got away with it. By now Il Duce's finest had had quite enough and four fighters came screaming after. They were much faster of course but not ready for the reception they got. He downed one and shot up another. When the Maryland finally touched tarmac, a section of ship's aerial was found jammed in the tail wheel assembly.

On his next trip four Macchi 200s came up to intercept. Undeterred, he found that, by dropping a wing flap, he could reduce speed and turning, force the much swifter fighters to over-fly. He brought down one of his pursuers and came back unscathed. Warby would become a symbol of Malta's astonishing resilience, an airborne D'Artagnan who either ignored the rules or broke them. With his glamorous girlfriend Christina Ratcliffe, the anti-social flyer became something of a local celebrity. The enemy just couldn't kill him though they tried very hard and he gave them every opportunity. On one mission he was posted as missing. He wasn't really, just diverted. In fact he'd popped over to occupied Greece, landed and picked up a cargo of contraband booze to keep the mess supplied!

The ugly duckling had become the beautiful swan. One of his crew left this pen portrait, glimpsed during a very tricky mission over Tripoli: 'He had his hat on top of his helmet, cigarette hanging from his lips; one elbow resting on the side of the cockpit, driving the plane with the other hand. His complete lack of fear and nonchalant attitude to the noise and from the flak was fantastic. Warby at his best…'

Warburton graduated from Marylands to stripped-down Beaufighters and then a specially adapted photo reconnaissance Spitfire. In one of these he was pestered by an AA crew while photographing Lampedusa who insisted on shooting at him. The recce plane was unarmed so he couldn't return fire. On landing safely, he immediately commandeered a fully equipped fighter, took to the air again, sought out the offending Italians and blasted them into oblivion. Returning home, he went up again in the photo plane to ensure there was tangible evidence of the destruction.

The **Bristol Type 156 Beaufighter** ('Beau') was a wartime variant of the Beaufort Bomber introduced in 1940 as a twin-engined heavy fighter. Over 5,000 were built and the aircraft served in multiple roles throughout the war.

By October 1943, the pilot who had been written off as hopeless was commanding 336 PR Wing in North Africa and leading four squadrons. On 12 April 1944, he took off from the UK to undertake a PR mission deep into the heart of the Fatherland, as far south as Regensburg and Schweinfurt. He never came back, vanishing into the blue with a suitably mythical flourish. In August 2002, the remains of his P38 F-5B were unearthed in a field near Egling in South Germany where locals, who had been boys at the time, recalled seeing it come down in flames. Malta would go on to receive the George Cross and his name would be forever associated with it.

CHAPTER 4

WAR WITHOUT PITY

1941–45

> *Above the earth, on searchlight-silvered wings, rides death*
> *In his most awful form – the hand of war;*
> *And from the earth in shuddering cry goes up –*
> *Sirens – whistles – bells warn the world*
> *That death rides out with crosses on his wings.*

Sergeant F. Cremer, RAMC, September 1942, *Untitled*

BARELY 30 YEARS AFTER THE FOKKER SCOURGE, aerial warfare had changed beyond all recognition. On 6 and 9 August 1945 the Allies would drop two atomic bombs on Japan – Hiroshima and Nagasaki – 129,000 people died, the world changed and, in reality, the age of the fighter ace was over. Instead, weapons of mass destruction, delivering death and an abominable legacy of cancerous contagion would continue to blight succeeding generations. In this kind of war, there would be no winners, just Armageddon.

Operation *Barbarossa*

In the wee small hours of 22 June 1941, around 03.15, the Red Army, woefully ill-prepared, emasculated by relentless purges, found itself under attack. Hitler was launching Operation

Barbarossa – his master plan for the utter destruction of the Soviet regime. At the front, the *schwerpunkt*, came the Luftwaffe aiming to deliver the knockout blow to the Russian war machine just as the *panzers* began to roll. Accounts vary but the Russians may have lost 2,000 aircraft on the first day, double that by the end of the third. Göring admitted to losing 35. Germany had hegemony in the warm summer skies above the endless plains of Russia. But that was the problem. The Soviet Union really was endless and this contest, begun so one-sidedly, would end in the scorched ruins of Berlin.

Germany lost the war in the East. Yet, during much of the conflict, the Luftwaffe enjoyed considerable superiority in the air. Her aces racked up astonishing scores, a vastly higher kill ratio than they would ever achieve in the West. Hitler's pilots were better trained than their Soviet opponents and, for much of the time, flew superior aircraft. The old 'hunter' mentality was still active: the German ideal of the predatory ace whose primary function was to shoot down enemies and compete for scores against his comrades. This pre-war generation of young Germans had been brought up to think of themselves as racially superior. The early *Barbarossa* victories, breathtaking in scale, appeared to validate the myth.

One of the top-scorers was Walter 'Nowi' Nowotny who amassed a cull of 258, all but three of which were over the Eastern Front. He came from a small town in Lower Austria, his father a railway official. Clearly, the family liked uniforms as two brothers both joined the Wehrmacht. One of them would die at Stalingrad. At school Walter was keen on sports while still finding time to sing in a convent choir.

Already a paid-up party member, he enlisted in October 1939 and had earned his wings by the time *Barbarossa* kicked off. One of his pals was Paul Galland, Adolf's younger brother, an ace in his own right before the RAF killed him. Nowotny was assigned to 9 Staffel of JG 54 – known as the Devil's Squadron. Here he was mentored by hard-bitten flyers who had already seen a fair bit of action. Mostly he would fly a Fw 190 or Me 109 and latterly, the first jet fighter the Me 262. His first active sorties over Russia were in the Me 109 but he had to wait till his 24th mission before he drew blood, bringing down a pair of ageing Soviet biplanes, though a third one did for him. He was forced to ditch in the Gulf of Riga and spend three miserable days in his dinghy before making it to a friendly shore. The trousers he wore when shot down (*abschusshose*) became a form of sartorial talisman and he continued to wear them for every sortie. He was soon back in the air and on form, claiming a flying boat and Ilyushin DB-3 bomber.

By July 1942, he'd earned his Luftwaffe Honour Goblet – a fine huntsman's trophy awarded after he bagged his 30th kill. On 20 July he downed five more. After adding another triple kill on 2 August he nearly came to grief when attempting victory rolls in an already shot-up Me 109, his plane somersaulting rather more savagely than he'd intended. This got him his Knight's Cross. In September, with a tally of 56, he was granted some home leave in Vienna, the last occasion he'd see his brother Hubert. Axis fortunes in the east were about to change. It wasn't until after the ring closed on von Paulus' doomed army that he first flew a Fw 190. He liked the plane and stepped up his already high kill rate, averaging two Russian aircraft per day and continuing for weeks on end.

His flying circus of aces, Karl Schnorrer, Anton Dobele and Rudolf Rademacher, formed the *Teufelskette* – 'Devil's Swarm'. These were the elite, the four musketeers of the clouds. Over the course of the conflict their collective score totalled 524. Nobody else in any combatant air arm came anywhere near. On his 344th sortie on 5 June 1943, he notched up his 100th victory, no 42 of the Luftwaffe to do so. By August he was made up to group commander (*Gruppenkommandeur*) and, in that month alone, shot down another 49, his score now standing at 161.

During September he downed ten in two sorties and earned Oak Leaves on his Knight's Cross. The Fuhrer himself was due to present the decoration on 22 September though by then he'd pushed his total bag to 215. He was now top gun in the Luftwaffe – the ace of aces. He'd more than doubled von Richthofen's record. He soon had Swords added to his Oak Leaves and the ceremony due on the 22nd was up-graded accordingly. On 14 October, he became the first Axis ace to achieve 250 kills. A grateful Führer telephoned him to say he'd been awarded Diamonds on top of his Oak Leaves and Swords. In Nazi Germany they did not come any higher. Only 27 members of their armed forces earned this ultimate accolade.

The actual award ceremony took place at Rastenburg, the Wolf's Lair, Hitler's eastern redoubt. But the swarm's days were numbered. On 11 November Dobele was killed in a mid-air collision with a Russian fighter. Schnorrer suffered serious injuries next day when forced to bail out too low. A mere three days after that 'Nowi' was taken off combat missions – he was too valuable to lose. He was promoted to air commodore and sent on a PR tour through Germany and Austria, receiving civic awards in his home city of Vienna. He was still only 23.

As the Battle for Normandy ended in total defeat and the whole German position in the west seemed to be unravelling, Nowotny was given command of his own kommando. Based near Osnabrück this most elite of elite units would be flying one

The **Messerschmitt Me 262** was the world's first jet fighter to fly, ahead of the Allies. It was both faster and better armed than anything Britain and the United States had to put up against it. Work on the design had begun before the war but the aircraft didn't enter service till mid-1944. The engines were subject to repeated mechanical problems and supplies of aviation fuel were running out by the end of the war. Providentially it came too late to affect the war's outcome, although Me 262s shot down over 500 Allied planes.

of Hitler's wonder weapons that would change the tide of war now running so heavily against him. It wasn't just that they'd be flying the new jet-propelled Me 262s but they'd be testing them too. Rushed into production, the new miracle fighters were far from trouble free. Still, on 7 October, his old skills still holding, Nowotny downed a B-24 Liberator.

Adolf Galland was one of those charged with supervising the jets' performance. He wasn't impressed; they just weren't living up to their hype. The pilots weren't that happy either but that did not prevent some, including General Keller, Galland's fellow inspector, from attributing the failures to a lack of grit on the aces' part – the Luftwaffe just wasn't what it had been. On 8 November both senior officers were at Nowotny's command post and the USAAF obligingly organised a bombing raid to coincide. Two pairs of Me 262s prepared to go up and intercept. Nowi went with them. Only two got off the ground at the first attempt, Nowotny's turbines refused to fire up and he finally got into the air without his wingman.

By now the initial pair had aborted after taking hits and Nowotny flew on to his *Gotterdammerung* alone. For the only time, he wasn't wearing his lucky trousers. His first radio call was to announce he had shot down another Liberator and a P-51. Soon though he was calling in engine trouble and then they received a last garbled transmission. Its content is still disputed – did he say he had an onboard fire or the plane was burning? The truth remains shrouded. Whether mechanical failure or enemy fire got him can't be confirmed.

A few US pilots have laid claim to bringing down the great Olympian but these kills remain unsubstantiated. Witnesses simply saw his plane shriek down in a vertical dive and smash into the earth, a suitably Wagnerian flourish. Nowi Nowotny was buried in Vienna, his pallbearers some of the Reich's greatest surviving aces. Galland delivered the eulogy. His grave was a place of honour in the city until 2003, when the Austrian government decided to strip his resting place of the distinction.

By June 1941, Nazi aces had been tested and hardened in the cauldrons of Spain, Poland, France and over Britain. Soviet forces in contrast had not, and had been bled white by Stalin's maniac purges. Anyone with any talent had been eliminated; tactical doctrines, training and kit were woefully inadequate. By the time Russia began the catching-up process in 1942 a cadre of German flyers was emerging, many of whom had flown 500 or more sorties, and whose combat experience vastly exceeded anything seen before or since. Combat fatigue would always be an element but some who switched to fighting over Normandy would have had a thousand sorties in the east under their belts. Some, such as ace Alfred Grislawski, with over 800 missions and 132 skills remained supremely confident: 'By that time (summer 1944) I could master any situation, and when I entered air combat I could tell in advance whom I was going to shoot down.'

During September 1942, German ace Herman Graf brought down over three-score Soviet planes, ten in just one day, scores never equalled in the west. As the Soviets increasingly got back into the game after 1942, Graf noted that many aces arriving from the west found their opposition unexpectedly as tough as the RAF:

> Hahn [Hans Robert 'Assi' Hahn, over 100 victories] … told me that the air combats are not easier, but instead harder than what he previously had experienced. He, who is used to merciless air combats against a skilful enemy over the English Channel, told us that he had to mobilize all his skills to fight enemies who proved to be at least as skilful as the Englishmen. Artur Gärtner (27 kills) flying with JG 54 confirmed; Those 'Kanaljäger' arrived to us and thought that it was an easy game on the Russian Front. Well, they soon learned that this was not the case.

One of those 'star' Luftwaffe pilots was Otto Kittel. From Silesia in the old Austria-Hungary and born in 1917, Kittel joined the air force in 1939 in time for the outbreak of war. He first flew in earnest during the very short *blitz* of unlucky Yugoslavia. Now he found himself flying in support of Army Group North, driving towards Leningrad. *Barbarossa* was barely 28 hours old when he downed a pair of Tupolev SB-2 bombers. His score rose relentlessly, 19 within his first year and 39 by the middle of February 1943. Despite his and the brilliance of others, the tide had already turned. Stalingrad had been a major disaster and blustering Hermann Göring had failed to make good his boast that he could supply the encircled army from the air.

That spring Kittel fought in blue Russian skies over the Crimea, Vitebsk, Kharkov and Kursk – Operation *Citadel*, an ill-judged bid to regain some initiative by eliminating the great salient. On 14 September he claimed his 100th kill. Remarkable as this was, he was the 53rd Luftwaffe ace to top the century. This feat earned him the coveted Knight's Cross of the Iron Cross. Oak Leaves were added in the spring of 1944 when he'd racked up another 50 victories and the award was made personally by Hitler at his alpine lodge, the Berghof, on 5 May.

In the same month his unit was shifted westwards as the inevitability of an Allied amphibious landing loomed large and attacks on the Fatherland gained momentum. In August he was promoted to squadron leader and scored his 200th success. This time it was to be the Knight's Cross with Oak Leaves and Swords. By the winter months of early 1945, the Luftwaffe was losing the battle on both fronts. Either on 14 or 16 February (the precise date is disputed), Kittel went up in his Fw 190 to take on a flock of Sturmovik over the Courland pocket. This was what was left of Army Group North, holding the Courland Peninsula. Details are unclear but his plane went down in flames. Aces are never immortal.

In the east the Russians flew in relatively small formations compared to the much larger units the USAAF would be deploying over Germany from 1943. The Luftwaffe tended to attack from the vantage of height; the Me 109 could out-climb its Soviet rivals and escape easily from a dogfight. The Germans were the hunters, they chose the time and ground. The Soviets, like the RAF before 1940, were mired in the archaic and vulnerable three-plane vic flight pattern. Their communications were inferior; they could only receive, and not transmit as well. Nobody could say the Russians lacked grit and, in the air as on the ground below, they showed extraordinary courage and resilience. Their losses at the outset had been catastrophic; any other air force would have been utterly crushed.

Erich Rudorffer was another German ace who flew throughout the entire war, scoring 222 kills to become the seventh most successful ace of all time. Unusually, he survived to a ripe old age, dying in 2016 at 98. He fought in all theatres, flew over a thousand combat missions, fought 300 dogfights, was shot down 16 times and jumped nine. His all-time record was 13 kills in 17 minutes – pretty impressive even by Luftwaffe standards.

The White Rose of Stalingrad

It wasn't all entirely one-sided. Russia produced some high-scoring aces. Aleksandr Poktyshin knocked down 59 of the Luftwaffe flying a P-39 Aircobra, generally regarded as a very poor second to the Me 109 and certainly to the Fw 190. Boris Safonov won the first 16 of his victories in an outmoded I-16 Ishak. What might he have done with a Spitfire and radar support? Russian tactics did not place the same emphasis on scoring, their

The **Ilyushin Il-2 Sturmovik** or 'Ilyusha' was a single-engined, two-man ground-attack aircraft introduced in 1941. It spearheaded the revival of Soviet fortunes in the air. Robust and reliable – in all variants over 42,000 were produced, making the Sturmovik arguably the most piloted plane of all time.

Lydia Litvyak, 1942.

job was to attack the invader anywhere and anyhow. Ground strafing missions were perceived by German aviators as menial whilst the Red Air Force punished the Wehrmacht harder and harder as it struggled across the vastness of the steppe.

Soviet women took on combat roles too, initially organised into three all-female regiments; then, increasingly, distributed amongst other units as they proved their worth. The most famous was the 588th Night Bomber Regiment – known as 'night witches' because of the whooshing sound their engines made in stealth mode as they neared their targets.

The Germans loathed and feared them. Any German pilot who downed a 'witch' was automatically awarded an Iron Cross. Among their number were the world's first female air aces – Katya Budanova (1916–43) and Lydia Litvyak (1921–43). Both would become famous in the fighting over Stalingrad. They would end their careers serving with the elite 9th Guards, a regiment composed only of aces or potential aces.

Both flew the Yakovlev Yak-1 aircraft, transferring regiments a number of times to stay with the same plane. Budanova had 11 air victories, Litvyak 16. The latter performed her first solo flight at 15 and became a flight instructor. Like so many other Soviet aviators, her family had suffered in Stalin's purges – her father had disappeared in 1937.

Sources vary regarding Budanova's first kills. Her mechanic, Inna Pasportnikova, wrote that she shot down her first aircraft on 6 October when she attacked 13 Ju 88 bombers, downing one. Two Messerschmitt Bf 110s followed in December. In the following months she was credited with several more.

By June 1943 Budanova had six victories to her credit; heavy air combat raised that to 11. On 19 July 1943 she flew her last mission, near Novokrasnovka. That morning she was involved in a dogfight with Me 109s. Inna Pasportnikova later recalled:

> She spotted three Messerschmitts going on the attack against a group of bombers. Katia attacked and diverted the enemy. A desperate fight developed in the air. Katia managed to pick up an enemy aircraft in her sight and riddle him with bullets. This was the fifth aircraft she killed personally. Katia's fighter rapidly soared upward and swooped down on a second enemy aircraft. She 'stitched' it with bullets, and the second Messer, streaming black smoke, escaped to the west. But Katia's red starred fighter had been hit; tongues of flame were already licking at the wings.

Budanova managed to put out the fire and force-landed in no man's land. By the time local farmers found her, she was already dead. They buried her on the outskirts of the village.

Litvyak loved flowers, she put them in her cockpit and painted white lilies on her plane. That was why the Soviet press referred to her as the 'White Lily of Stalingrad', translated in the West as 'The White Rose'. She scored her first two kills on 13 September, three days after her arrival and on her third mission to cover Stalingrad. That day, four Yak-1s attacked a formation of Junkers escorted by Messerschmitts. First she took on a Ju 88 which fell in flames, then went after a Me 109G-2 'Gustav' on the tail of her squadron commander, Raisa Beliaeva.

German pilot Staff Sergeant Erwin Maier parachuted from his aircraft, was captured by Soviet troops, and asked to see the Russian ace who had outflown him. When he met Litvyak, he thought he was the butt of a joke.

By February she had been awarded the Order of the Red Star, made a junior lieutenant and selected as an '*okhotniki*'. These free hunters were pairs of experienced pilots allowed to search for targets at will. Twice, she was forced to land her damaged Yak. On 22 March she was flying as part of a group of six Yak fighters when they attacked a dozen Junkers. Litvyak shot down one of the bombers, but was in turn attacked and wounded by the escorts. She managed to shoot down a Messerschmitt before returning to ground

Wounded again in July after six Yaks encountered 30 German bombers, she downed one before making a forced landing. Refusing medical leave, she went on to knock out two more fighters within a week.

Litvyak did not return to base after her fourth sortie of the day on 1 August 1943. Two Messerschmitts dived while she was attacking a group of bombers. Pilot Ivan Borisenko recalled:

> Lily just didn't see the Messerschmitt 109s flying cover … A pair of them dived on her and when she did see them she turned to meet them. Then they all disappeared behind a cloud.

Borisenko saw her a last time, through a gap in the clouds, her Yak-1 pouring smoke and pursued by as many as eight Germans. No parachute was seen, no explosion, yet she never returned. Soviet authorities suspected that she had been

The **Bell P-39 Aircobra** was designed pre war but came into service with American air forces in 1941. It had an innovative engine arrangement, with only a single-stage, single-speed supercharger. Although it under-performed at altitudes above 17,000 feet, it remained an effective ground-attack plane, popular with Soviet forces. Over 9,500 were produced.

captured. That labelled her a potential traitor – she was denied a posthumous medal.

Seeking justice, Pasportnikova embarked on a 36-year search for her landing place. In 1979, after uncovering more than 90 other crash sites and 30 aircraft she learned that an unidentified woman pilot had been buried in the village of Dmitrievka. A commission determined that Litvyak had been killed in action after sustaining a head wound. On 6 May 1990, President Gorbachev finally declared Lydia Litvyak a Hero of the Soviet Union.

Empire of the Sun

'A day that will live in infamy' was how President Franklin D. Roosevelt labelled the Japanese attack on Pearl Harbor on 7 December 1941. It was a very bad day for the United States. Several capital ships were sunk or badly damaged. Casualties were high. But, the vital but, the Japanese missed the American carriers, which meant any savouring of victory turned to ashes. By the time the war in the Far East ended, much of Japan would look very similar.

Short of natural resources the Japanese military government proposed to create a vast imperial shield around their home islands, harvesting the resources of Burma, Malaya, the Dutch East Indies and the Philippines. The war they unleashed would spread over a vast canvas and involve desperate fighting as American forces 'island-hopped', taking back bastion after bastion as the ring closed abound the Empire of the Sun.

One of the highest-scoring US aces in the Pacific theatre was Major Richard Ira Bong. A child of Swedish immigrants, he had been a student teacher in his native Wisconsin when he joined a civil aviation training scheme. At the end of May 1941 he joined the Army Air Corps, gaining his wings early next year, after the United States had joined the war. While on home service in California he flew the P-38 Lightning. His barn-storming antics, such as lapping the Golden Gate Bridge, got him temporarily grounded. This cost him his passage to England but, after transferring to 84 Squadron, he shipped out to the Pacific.

In September 1942, Bong was based in Darwin with the 'Flying Knights' of 9 Squadron. He soon moved to Port Moresby to support Australian and American forces engaged in the murderous campaign along the Kokoda Trail. There, on 27 December, he shot down two Japanese planes – first blood and a Silver Star. In March 1943 he made first lieutenant and that summer brought down anther quartet of Zeros, receiving the Distinguished Service Cross and, in August becoming a captain. His P-38 was named 'Marge' after his girlfriend Marge Vattendahl and its nose adorned with her image. By the spring of 1944, his score had climbed to 27, passing World War I top scorer Eddie Rickenbacker. He was now a major.

After a spell of home leave that spring, he came back to New Guinea and a staff post. He wasn't ready just to fly a desk and resumed combat sorties, racking his score up to 40. Despite his proficiency, he considered himself a poor shot and invariably closed to point-blank range, often charging through the debris spewed from his victim. In December 1944, he won the Medal of Honor and, very soon after, a permanent home posting. His shooting war was over. Major Richard Bong was killed during a test flight in the USA on the very same day the first atomic bomb was dropped.

Admiral Isoroku Yamamoto was head of the Japanese Imperial Navy and architect of Pearl Harbor. Unsurprisingly he was on America's most wanted list. They got their chance in April 1943. Having cracked Japanese codes, American intelligence knew the ever precise Yamamoto would be on a routine inspection to a small island called Ballale, off the south coast of Bougainville at 09.45 on the 18th. US Army P-38 Lightnings flying from Guadalcanal had sufficient range for an intercept.

Major John W. Mitchell, commanding 339th Fighter Squadron, chose 18 of his best pilots for the mission. Four planes would actually take down Yamamoto's bomber aircraft while the rest fought off his fighter escort which was bound to be substantial. The attackers would have to cover a distance of 435 miles skimming the waves to avoid detection, relying solely on impeccable compass-aided navigation. If they got it right, evading Japanese ears and eyes, they should be in the target zone by 09.35, ready and waiting.

Their intended victim was famously punctual. The intruders' flight would be a five-stage, two and three quarter hour marathon and should allow them to bounce their target 30 miles from Ballale. Two of the US raiders had to abort, 16 screamed into the attack. Mitchell had got his calculations of time and speed spot on – the Japanese were totally surprised. Yamamoto was bang on time with six Zeroes as his escort.

The Lightnings were still just above the water when they spotted their quarry 4,500 feet above. Of the four-plane 'hit' flight, one experienced difficulties and had to pull out, taking his wingman with him. The two remaining Lightnings, flown by Captain Thomas Lanphier and Lieutenant Rex Barber kept going. In the furious melée only one P-38 was destroyed while two of the Japanese Bettys, one carrying Yamamoto, and half of

The **Lockheed P-38 Lightning** (known as the 'fork-tailed devil') was a highly successful twin-engined heavy fighter with distinctive twin boom and a central nacelle. It came into service in the summer of 1941. It was the start of a 25-year career which would see it become the mainstay of American air forces in the Far East until superseded (though never totally replaced) by the P-51 Mustang. Over 10,000 were built.

their Zeroes went down. Both Lanphier and Barber claimed the kill, a fracas that raged on for half a century. For the Japanese, Yamamoto's death was a massive blow.

Thomas McGuire was brought up in Florida, joining up as an air cadet in July 1941. He'd become a close second to Bong in terms of top scores – his final tally was 38. From time to time his wingman was no less a legend than Charles Lindbergh (whom he appears to have treated rather disdainfully). Most of McGuire's early training was done in Texas and he first flew in anger over the distant Aleutians – a forgotten corner of the vast Pacific canvas. Like Bong he became familiar with the formidable P-38 and was blooded over New Guinea. It wasn't until August 1943 that, flying shotgun for bombers raiding Wewak in New Guinea, he shot down three Japanese aircraft. Next day he added another brace to that week's bag, an ace in 48 hours.

His luck very nearly ran out during that autumn. Still in New Guinea, he was scrambled to intercept bombers and their Zero escorts. A dogfight sprawled over Oro Bay. Spotting a Lightning, already damaged, being mauled by a pack of Jap fighters, he waded in. He accounted for three of them but had to jump after sustaining hits. As he struggled to free the canopy and bail out,

The **Mitsubishi A6M Zero** was the standard Japanese fighter of the war, coming into service in July 1940. Over 10,000 were constructed and, at the outset of the war in the Far East, performed very well. Their legendary agility in a dogfight led to high kill ratios over inexperienced American pilots. It quickly became outdated and outclassed by new Allied planes. It was the aircraft of choice for the *Kamikazes*.

his 'chute harness stuck and he became trapped. He stayed that way as the plane spiralled down from 12,000 feet. At 1,000 feet he finally pulled free and ditched into the sea. He was rescued by a patrol boat but had damage to his wrist and ribs which needed six weeks' hospitalisation. He won both a Silver Star and a Purple Heart, together with promotion to captain soon after.

During 1944, he rose from major to operations officer for 475th Fighter Group. By 7 January 1945, he was only two kills behind Bong – and keen to surpass him. That morning he went up in a flight of four P-38s, flying over Negros Island in the central Philippines. The quartet was looking for trade. They bounced a couple of Japanese aerodromes in the hope of stirring the hornets' nest but only a single Oscar came up to fight. One of the flight came under attack, and his wingman manoeuvred to cover him.

The lone Oscar was flown by Warrant Officer Akira Sugimoto, no slouch with many hours' flying time. He turned his attentions towards McGuire and his wingman, Edwin Weaver. Weaver took evasive action as the Oscar fastened onto his tail, McGuire attempting to distract Sugimoto. As the planes closed the American increased the angle of his turn. The aircraft were flying at only 300 feet – precisely the kind of tactic McGuire had denigrated in his manual, *Combat Tactics in the Southwest Pacific Area*. Rightly so. His P-38 stalled, then, laden with drop tanks, crashed into the scrub. His body was recovered by locals and returned to the United States four years later, to be interred at Arlington.

Chasing Bong and McGuire was Charles 'Mac' MacDonald. He was older, born in 1914 and came into the Army Air Corps as a graduate entry in 1938, gaining both his wings and a commission in late May the following year. He was at Pearl Harbor the day the dive-bombers came. After a number of stateside postings he joined 475th Fighter Group at Dobodura in New Guinea on 1 October 1943. Once there he didn't waste time, scoring his first four kills that month and qualifying as an ace in November. He was made up to lieutenant colonel the day after and group commander shortly after. His final tally was 27 Japanese planes destroyed. He had a busy post-war career and retired as a full colonel in 1961.

Operation *Overlord*

On the night of 5/6 June 1944, the largest armada ever assembled crossed the English Channel, their target the Calvados coast of Normandy. This would be the great breach of Hitler's European empire. Only four years since the Allies were chased out of Dunkirk they were coming back. This was the greatest, most complex amphibious operation of all time, the most profound and ambitious since Agamemnon and his bronze-clad Achaeans had set sail for Troy over 3,000 years earlier. Control of the skies was everything. By now the Luftwaffe, though by no means a spent force, was severely weakened by the steady attrition of the Eastern Front, the nemesis of Hitler's thousand-year Reich.

The **North American Aviation P-51 Mustang** was a US single-seat long-range fighter, one of the most successful designs of World War II. It first flew for the RAF in January 1942 and by late 1943 had become the escort for bombing raids over Germany where it provided much-needed fighter power. Robust, reliable, powerfully armed with six .50 calibre Brownings, it was a driver of Allied air superiority in 1944 and remained in service with world air forces for another 30 years. Over 15,000 were built.

One of those who flew over North-West Europe in this last and greatest crusade was American flyer Chuck Yeager. A post-war legend, he had enlisted as a private in September 1941, soon qualifying as a mechanic. In peacetime Yeager was both too young and his education seemingly too lacking to allow him to try for pilot's wings. What he did possess were lightning reflexes and incredibly sharp eyesight. After Pearl Harbor, requirements were relaxed – he qualified in March 1943. A stunt that involved flying so low he pruned a local farmer's trees got him temporarily grounded, but didn't damage his career and that November he shipped out for England.

A reconnaissance Spitfire over Normandy, 1944.

Based at RAF Leiston, 363d Fighter Squadron flew P-51 Mustangs. He christened his plane 'Glamorous Glen' after the future Mrs Yeager – Glennis Faye Dickhouse. He notched up two kills before being brought down over France on 5 March 1944. The mission flew over Bordeaux with Yeager flying in the unenviable 'tail end Charlie' position. Then:

> Three Fw 190s came in from the rear and cut my elevator cables; I snap-rolled with the rudder and jumped at 18,000 feet. I took off my dinghy-pack, oxygen mask, and helmet in the air; and then, as I was whirling on my back and began to feel dizzy, I pulled the ripcord at 8,000 feet. An Fw 190 dove at me, but when he was about 2,000 yards from me a P-51 came in on his tail and blew him to pieces.

He wasn't out of the woods, in fact he was about to come down in one but not before one of the Germans dived to machine-gun him in his harness. Saved by another P-51 which nailed the Focke-Wulf:

> I landed into a forest-clearing in which there was a solitary sapling about twenty feet tall. I grabbed the top of the sapling as I passed it and swung gently to the ground. My chute was hung up in the tree; however, I hid my 'Mae West' and started off to the south-east, for I thought that I was in the forbidden zone. Before I had gone 200 feet half a dozen Frenchmen ran up to me. Some of them got my chute down, and one of the men took me by the arm and led me to a house some 200 yards away. There I was given food and civilian clothes. A gendarme was seen approaching the house at this moment, and so I was quickly hidden in the barn. When the gendarme left I was brought back into the house where one of the men who had left the group now returned and gave me a note in English telling me to trust the people in whose hands I was. I was then taken to another house about a kilometer away, and from there my journey was arranged.

This was the start of a series of adventures as the young pilot was passed along an established escape line at great risk to his saviours. He wasn't just a bystander though; he trained some of his guardians in bomb-making. Yeager made it out to Gibraltar, helping a disabled fellow escapee en route. Back in the war barely two months after being shot down, his exploit won him a Bronze Star.

High Command had a rule that prohibited evaders from flying over occupied territory again. Yeager successfully petitioned Eisenhower to relax the stricture. D-Day had now taken place and the resistors were openly taking on the occupiers. They would be at less risk of compromise if he were brought down again. The supreme commander concurred and Yeager flew over France once more. It was a good call on Ike's part. On 12 October Yeager racked up five victories, to become an 'ace in a day'. He nailed two of these without firing a single round. Lining up a Bf 110 in his sights, the German panicked, banked and collided with his own wingman, destroying them both.

A different kind of threat required a different breed of ace. The Blitz was long over and the RAF/USAAF together were approaching hegemony in the skies. But Hitler still had a card to play. The V-1 and, latterly V-2 bombs, presaged an altogether new aerial warfare – the bomber that might always get through, a strategic nightmare. Once developed at Peenemunde, thousands of V-1s – doodlebugs – were flung into the skies from French and Dutch launch sites, creating an added imperative for *Overlord*.

From June to late October 1944, over 9,000 were launched, primarily against London and the south-east of England. Essentially a terror weapon, they came too late to swing the balance back in the Axis' favour. On average, the doodlebugs flew at 340 mph and at just over 3,000 feet. Only fighters with first-class low-altitude capabilities could catch them. Happily Britain had the Hawker Tempest, but in small numbers – only 30 to begin with, assigned to 150 Wing. Their task was to intercept the V-1 before it reached the target area and destroy it mid-air – no easy matter.

One technique, calling for tremendous nerve, harnessed the airflow over the Tempest's wing to lift one of the doodlebug's stubby fins. To do it meant manoeuvring the Tempest's wing a

The **Focke-Wulf Fw 190 Würger** was a single-seat German fighter which came into service in the summer of 1941. It was a plane favoured by many German aces, especially on the Eastern Front. Like the Me 109 it was a mainstay of the Luftwaffe's fighter fleets and, at the time outclassed the Spitfire Mark V. It wasn't until the Mark IX that the Spitfire caught up (although always more manoeuvrable). Over 20,000 Fw 190s were built during the war.

scant six inches below. Done right this would tip the flying bomb and disrupt its gyro mechanism. The beastly thing would then go into an uncontrolled dive, hopefully to explode harmlessly on impact.

This 'aerodynamic flip' stunt was first employed by Major R. E. Turner of 356th Fighter Group (USAAF), flying a P-51 on 18 June. By late summer there were a hundred Tempests flying, soon joined by stripped-down P-47M Thunderbolts. Spitfires, Mosquitoes and some P-51s were also adapted. During those long summer days, even at night the flying bombs were easy to detect from the loudness of their rocket-powered engines and trailing exhaust plumes. Wing Commander Roland Beaumont set the sights on his 20mm cannon to converge on them at 300 yards. It would become the norm – he shot down 31 doodlebugs.

These sorties (dubbed 'diver' patrols) were as tricky as any foray against a manned fighter or bomber. The V-1's thick steel casing rendered the hull near bulletproof. Only an exploding cannon round would do the job and the blast when the thing went up could easily engulf the fighter. Nonetheless, a handful of V-1 aces emerged. Squadron Leader Joseph Berry from 501 Squadron destroyed 59, becoming top gun. A Belgian, Squadron

The **Hawker Tempest** was a development of the highly successful Typhoon which wrought havoc on Axis targets during the Normandy battle. The Tempest was fast and powerful, sporting two 20mm under-wing cannon, long barrels projecting menacingly. It proved handy against doodlebugs and went on to launch ground attacks in support of *Market Garden*. Blitzing German airfields, it could even, at lower altitudes, take on the Me 262.

Leader Remy van Lierde (264 Squadron) got 44 outright and shared another nine. By the end, the Mosquitoes had downed 623, Spitfires, 303 and Mustangs, 232.

This was indeed a new type of warfare: the V-2, a true missile, proved impossible to stop. Britain was fortunate: they came too late and were relatively ineffective even if they were psychologically terrifying. Some jet fighters, the Gloster Meteor, for example, did engage V-2s but only brought down 13 of them. Jets were the shape of things to come – future dogfights in the post-war world would be between jet-powered fighters.

Mustangs over Berlin

When I saw mustangs over Berlin, I knew the jig was up.

Hermann Göring

The fat man was right, the game was pretty much up and the P-51 was a major player. The Allied bombing campaign, underway from 1943, had inflicted colossal damage and loss of life. It also cost the lives of many bomber crews. Providing adequate fighter cover over Germany was impossible as British and American aircraft simply did not have the range. But, with long-range tanks fitted, the Mustang did. That was the game changer. Initially the fighters were tied to the bombers' apron strings. As the raiders took off, first tier protection was afforded by P-38s and 47s, which turned back as their fuel was expended and handed over to Mustangs. Keeping station with the bombers meant the fighters had little time to react when the Luftwaffe pounced above their threatened fatherland.

Lumbering Bf-110s, well-armed but far too slow, were easy meat. The versatile Fw 190A, laden with additional armament, performed badly at extreme heights. The Me 109 did rather better at altitude but couldn't really carry greater firepower. Neither was a match for the Mustang. Luftwaffe tactics consisted of a big wing of fighters, lined up like rugby forwards, ready to charge full tilt into the Flying Fortresses, blasting through and scoring kills before the escorts could properly respond.

Doolittle had a response to this. Like the Germans in 1940, over Britain, he sent swarms of P-51s out ahead, unencumbered by shepherding duties, looking for a fight. They found plenty and within a week, the Luftwaffe had lost 17 per cent of its pilots, losses Germany could simply never hope to make good. Doolittle noted that 'Adolf Galland said the day we took our fighters off the bombers and put them against German fighters, Germany lost the war.' That may be a dash of hubris but the hit was still palpable.

Galland wasn't quite done yet. His response was the *Gefechtsverband* – a double-decked formation. Units of Fw 190As were bracketed between formations of Me 109Gs. The first were to fly ahead to take on the bombers while the latter sparred with the escort. On paper this was pretty ingenious – sometimes it worked. If the 109s could get loose amongst the Liberators and Flying Fortresses delivering their rear-end attacks

James 'Jimmy' Doolittle (1896–1993) became justly famed for the 'Doolittle' Raid over Japan, launched in the wake of Pearl Harbor. Although strategically insignificant it was a tremendous morale booster and gave the enemy a taste of the whirlwind to come. He commanded Eighth Air Force in England and his shift in fighter tactics was a major innovation. After VE Day, Eighth Air Force began transferring to Okinawa but was saved further fighting when the war in the Far East ended.

at close range – 100 yards or less – bomber losses could be heavy. Often this proved impossible as the whole formation got entangled in dogfights with the free-flying Mustangs. The once invincible Luftwaffe was on its uppers but its battle-scarred aces would go down fighting.

A friend of Chuck Yeager, Clarence 'Bud' Anderson joined as a pre-war air cadet in his native California. Commissioned into the air force in September 1942, as a flyer with 363 Squadron based at Leiston, he flew his Mustang (named 'Old Crow' after the liquor) on 116 combat missions. He claimed 16½ confirmed kills and went through it all without a scratch. He ended the war as a major, completed thirty years military service and flew over 100 types of aircraft.

Operation *Jackpot* targeted German fighters on the ground. Again, the ubiquitous Mustang proved effective, bouncing Axis aerodromes. This war of attrition, beginning in earnest early in 1944, was ultimately intended to win hegemony over the skies for the Allies once the invasion fleet set sail. It did the job. The Luftwaffe was not completely a spent force. German bombers still pounded Bastogne, part of Hitler's last gasp offensive in the West but the outcome was decided. It had really been decided in 1940 over England. Failure to crush the RAF was more than just a setback. It was the kiss of death.

CHAPTER 5

MiG ALLEY, DESERT SKIES AND STORMY SEAS

Post-1945

Who's for the game, the biggest that's played,
The red crashing game of a fight?
Who'll grip and tackle the job unafraid?
And who thinks he'd rather sit tight?

Jessie Pope, *Who's For the Game?*

TWO WORLD WARS HAD CONFIRMED THE vital role of aircraft, both fighters and bombers. Yet the pre-World War II assumption that strategic bombing could bring an enemy convincingly to their knees had proved a fallacy. Allied Lancasters and Flying Fortresses had wrought mighty havoc on Germany's infrastructure but the bombing campaign had not ensured the Axis defeat. Likewise with Japan it required the use of that most deadly weapon, the atomic bomb, to bring the Empire of the Sun down. Now the world trembled at the prospect of a doomsday weapon.

Fighter aircraft had again acted as bomber shields, inflicting significant damage and casualties on enemy ground forces. In both Britain and the now dominant United States of America the independent air arm survived and thrived. It was a time of innovation: the jet engine had taken the technology back to pushers over tractors, but in a form that the RFC would have found unrecognisable. Korea would be the new battleground – the aces over Asian skies would be duelling with novel technologies.

Korea

The Korean War, which erupted in June 1950, would drag on for three years and cost tens of thousands of lives. North Korea, a hard-line communist dictatorship (then as now), invaded the more democratic south. Britain and the United States, on behalf of the United Nations, intervened to save the new republic from extinction. A bold amphibious operation turned the tables and the North began to reel. But, as the Allies neared the border with China, Mao also interposed: it was the Allies' turn to stumble backwards. After the battle of the Imjin, it became a war of attrition. Both sides stayed pretty much where they were and remain so today, dug in along the 38th Parallel.

From the outset in Korea, command of the skies was vital. The North was equipped with Yak piston-engined fighters which fell in droves to roaring American Mustangs, British Seafires and Sea

Jets are reaction engines – they generate thrust by jet propulsion. Frank Whittle is credited with the prototype. His Gloster E28/39 first flew as early as May 1941 but his Gloster Meteor (the first true British jet fighter) didn't enter service with the RAF till July 1944. Germany too produced a successful design – the Me 262. It flew in combat but couldn't be produced in sufficiently large numbers to affect the outcome of the war.

Furies. Allied aircraft were instrumental in halting the seemingly unstoppable rush of North Korean forces. Bombers proved less effective, the primitive nature of local infrastructures and near-medieval logistics depriving them of useful targets. Despite the vast numbers of sorties flown, the United States scarcely dinted the capacity of the North Koreans, and, latterly, the Chinese, to re-supply.

Knocking down outmoded Yaks might have been fine sport but these were, by 1951, replaced with far more formidable MiG-15 jets. The fifty or so initially flown by Chinese and Russian pilots soon increased over eightfold. By the end of the war over 800 flew from safe (at least in theory) harbours north of the Yalu River. It was the turn of the Americans and British to be outclassed. Losses amongst bombers began to rise. The Sabre Jet changed the dynamic back, though they appeared in far fewer in number than the MiGs – barely 150 were deployed over Korea. Happily, the American pilots, in qualitative terms, were far better. Three squadrons of Sabres were stationed at the vast aerodrome of Kimpo, just a few miles west of Seoul. As ever the fighter pilots regarded themselves as the elite, though those engaged in ground attack and strafing were, statistically, at greater risk.

MiG madness

Despite new technology, the pattern of flying patrols was not so different from the days of the Western Front. Pilots would be given their assignments at early morning briefings – cover for bombing raids or combat patrols. Each plane taxied for take-off at three-second intervals, then swept skywards to fly at around 40,000 feet, half that height for bomber escort. Flying in the classic 'finger-four' formation, with number three in command but ready to fight in pairs; the new jets were a dream to fly. Quieter, more reliable than the older prop-driven planes, though fuel had to be watched. Careful conservation could extend an hour's air time by up to 30 minutes. The Sabres soon achieved near total dominance in the air and safeguarded Allied airbases from enemy attack.

'MiG Alley' became the duelling ground of choice for Korean War aces. This clearly defined combat zone covered the north-west of North Korea, with Korea Bay lying to the west. On the eastern flank the zone was defined by a line slanting between the Sui-ho Reservoir and the settlement at Huichon. The enemy would come up from a complex of communist air-bases at Antung in Manchuria and be over the disputed territory in minutes. It took the American pilots considerably longer – leaving them barely 20 minutes flying time in the hostile space. As a rule, they made good use of it.

Such was the clear superiority of the formidable Sabres that pilots developed a form of bloodlust or 'MiG madness'. One so afflicted was Major George Davis who, with a dozen kills, had become the top-scoring American ace. By February 1952, fellow flyers were commenting on his hunting obsession: 'George's main goal in life was to shoot down MiGs … he was dwelling on his score a lot.' On patrol during the 10th of that month, he led a force of 18 F-86s riding shotgun for fighter-bombers attacking ground targets.

This was uninspiring stuff for aces, so he took a four-finger flight up the Yalu River Valley, hoping to pick a fight. Somewhat

The **Mikoyan-Gurevich MiG-15** was one of the first successful swept-wing designs which entered service with the Soviets in 1949. Over 12,000 were built and the plane served with over 40 air forces.

reckless on two counts: firstly, he was in charge of the overall mission (so not expected to go off and play), and secondly, MiGs tended to take comfort in large numbers, 60–80 at times. He got lucky, and spotted a clutch of ten flying south-east. Even before the dogfight he had lost half his flight, one running out of oxygen had had to turn back, shepherded by another.

Undeterred, he and his sole wingman waded in, scattering the opposition like sheep, though not before Davis had racked up another kill. Speed and surprise enabled the two American pilots to take on the enemy successfully at odds of 5 to 1. The trick now was to break off and get clear. But Davis had another MiG in his sights. Sliding in behind he gave the enemy a burst and saw his engine spurt satisfyingly into flames; down the MiG went into a dive from which there'd be no coming back.

Davis had no time to gloat. He'd sacrificed speed, his main asset, to close with the kill. Two down still left eight and they had recovered from their surprise. He attempted to turn and engage a third potential victim. This was at 32,000 feet where any manoeuvre tended to be sluggish. A fourth MiG raked his cockpit: the stricken F-86 spiralled down to bond with the

A North Korean MiG-15.

landscape. There was no sign of a parachute.

Davis' final tally of 14 would be the highest score of the war. Posthumously, he was promoted to lieutenant colonel and awarded the Medal of Honor on account of his 'indomitable fighting spirit, heroic aggressiveness, and superb courage in engaging the enemy against formidable odds … rather than maintain his superior speed and evade the enemy fire being concentrated on him, he elected to reduce his speed and sought out still a third MiG-15'.

Major George Davis Jr.

Uncommon valour or plain daft, it's a moot point. Yet perhaps that's the dividing line between the true ace and also-ran. To become an ace, to aspire to that ultimate status necessarily involves risk, perhaps the kind of risks lesser mortals would blink at. Speed, daring and skill are the hallmarks of the breed. But it doesn't always work; every ace flies with the near-certainty that one day his luck will surely run out. For George Davis that day was 10 February 1950.

Possibly too, he was a victim of the very propagandist celebrity he'd helped to foster. These early knights of the jet age, like their Great War predecessors, became household names. Their shining, glorious jousting in the skies stood in marked contrast to a largely anonymous ground war that had descended into costly stalemate.

Davis wasn't unique. MiG madness was so contagious many pilots would take big risks with fuel just to prolong their span in the combat zone. 'Bingo' was the minimum fuel requirement needed to get safely home. You could gain some precious minutes of bingo by gliding part of the way back – engine off. From

30,000 feet the aircraft could, in theory anyway, glide nearly 70 miles without crashing. This got more exciting if your motor refused to play and didn't fancy re-starting for the landing run. These 'dead-stick' landings were commonplace, the pilots skilled enough to get away with it. Oddly enough, this practice, which should have been deprecated, was habitually winked at, proof of the flyer's aggressive spirit.

Over enemy ground

Another truly hawkish ace was Captain Robinson ('Robbie') Risner who'd racked up eight victories by the autumn of 1952. On 22 October, while flying cover for fighter-bombers, he flushed a quartet of MiGs and set off in hot pursuit along the broad valley of the Yalu. He was way over very hostile Manchuria by the time he got to grips and beat up the rear-end MiG, riddling its cockpit. The enemy somehow survived the incoming rounds and performed an acrobatic 'split-S', levelling out and literally skimming the hedgerows so low he kicked up dust from a dry wadi. This was a resourceful opponent who now braked in the hope of making the far faster Sabre overfly.

Risner executed a lazy roll and throttled back so he was flying parallel to his quarry, so close the adversaries could plainly see one another. Despite the hits he had taken the communist pilot was still full of fight and shook an angry fist at his tormentor. Risner had a surreal moment, 'like a movie', so close he could make out the stitching on the other man's leather flying helmet. Ducking and weaving, the chase stretched for another 30-odd miles all the way to the Chinese airfield at Ta-tung-kou. At 300 knots the MiG was weaving between the hangars, Risner and his wingman still on his tail. Finally, the American got off a well-timed burst, sheared a wing and sent his victim smashing into runway tarmac.

It wasn't totally one-sided. Chinese ack-ack and ground fire was spitting at the two American jets in their contemptuous sally over

Three Sabres flying over Korea in 1953.

the airfield. Lieutenant Logan, the wingman, was the unlucky one. Enemy shells punctured his fuel tank and he began to bleed out. Risner ordered him to shut down the engine and then tried, like a blunt-nosed shepherd, to literally shunt the wounded plane home. Oil and fuel were haemorrhaging from the shot-up plane, cascading over his canopy. Logan had no choice finally but to bale out. He didn't make it back; he dropped into water and was dragged down by his parachute harness. Risner ended up running completely out of fuel but managed a safe 'dead-stick' landing.

Protocol dictated neither of them should have crossed into Chinese airspace in the first place. Strictly *verboten*, the restriction was far more honoured in the breach than the observance. Not only were such provocations winked at, many planned missions were designed to overfly. Most kills by those aces that scored ten or more victories were made over Manchuria.

General Frank Everest, having seen clear evidence that his pilots were closing in on a Chinese aerodrome, angrily reprimanded the men for the sake of form. Then, more quietly, suggested that if they were going to overfly, they should make damn sure they'd switched of their IFF ('Identification Friend or Foe'). A young Sabre pilot, Lieutenant Michael DeArmond, was warned by his flight leader that anyone who veered north of the line would be court-martialled. The same officer then led his four F-86s well into Chinese territory and bagged a MiG. When the younger man was asked where the incident had occurred he seamlessly altered the geographical location to the right side of the border. He was immediately assured he had a bright future in the USAF!

Colonel Francis Gabreski, a star-studded ace of World War II, like Risner, chased his target clear down the runway at Antung to bring the Russian down right under the noses of his Chinese hosts. He got clear away and even had the temerity to execute a victory roll over the field just to ram home his message. High command expressed outward horror at these antics but buzzing the enemy tarmac at Antung was common practice; skimming along at barely roof height, waking the communists up with the shrieking crash of a sonic boom. This wasn't mere bravado; such tactics were a deliberate provocation, inviting the MiGs to seek retaliation.

Ground strafing of parked MiGs, whilst tempting, was frowned upon. An unfortunate precedent had been set early in the war when a pair of F-80 Shooting Star flyers became lost but strafed the first field they came to – which turned out to be Russian. Both were court-martialled. Soviet commander Georgy Lobov complained the Americans were constantly violating the frontier and pouncing as the MiGs lifted off – he lost 26 planes to such opportunistic tactics during the first half of 1952. Sabre jets would be poised high above the mouth of the Yalu River, waiting

Francis 'Gabby' Gabreski (1919–2002) was the most successful American ace of World War II with 34½ confirmed kills. He also fought in Korea; 15 of his 26 years in the air force were spent in operations, quite a track record.

just for the dust from take-off. Happily the gun camera evidence from attacking F-86s, which showed enemy planes being blitzed with their landing gear still extended, often just got lost.

Aces with clipped wings

American policy was not always consistent. Ace pilot Captain Joe McConnell was grounded for frequent violations by his immediate superior. But his superior's superior intervened and countermanded the order. It could get tighter when something got messy. In January 1953, as the stalemate on the ground continued, Lieutenant Colonel Edwin Heller, leading 16 Squadron, took them on a sortie into Manchuria. Wounded in a dogfight he had a broken arm and a broken plane, the controls were out and the ejector mechanism u/s (unserviceable). The plane spun into a very long downward spiral toppling from 40,000 feet. Desperately, the wounded man attempted to claw a way out through his shattered canopy. G-forces and the screaming, arctic wind lent a hand; he was sucked clear. He bounced off the horizontal stabiliser and broke a leg to add to his injuries.

He survived the parachute drop but was captured and spent 28 months in a Chinese prisoner-of-war camp, not somewhere anybody would want to be. It was also enormously embarrassing. The incident provided glorious propaganda for the communists as the endless peace talks at Panmunjon dragged on. Worse, Swiss observers, en route to the talks, had a grandstand view of F-86s doing their stuff way north of the Yalu River. They added their condemnation to the chorus. American commanders had to take action.

In four days, 21–24 January 1953, Captain Dolph Overton brought down five MiGs. This was pretty impressive, even if all of his kills were scored way north of the border. The captain had been on a visit to a US radar installation at Cho-do and had observed the holding patterns of enemy planes waiting to land.

Cannily, he took station above the area flying a racetrack pattern. A racetrack pattern is not dissimilar to a holding pattern but the objective is to reduce visibility, say by sunlight slanting off your wings or fuselage. It limits manoeuvre and, consequently, the risk of detection. He turned off his IFF, attempting to hoodwink enemy radar into mistaking him for a friendly. Keeping his plane between the sun and his victims, he closed undetected at their 'six o'clock' position. Like von Richthofen he pounced, not relying on the F-86 radar-ranging sights. He picked off all five of his kills before they even knew he was there.

If Overton was expecting a hero's welcome, he was to be sadly disappointed. Instead, he was summoned to his commanding officer's office. Questioned as to where he'd been flying, he answered truthfully. His superior, Colonel Mitchell, knew this perfectly well of course but he was under pressure. The ace found himself grounded, stripped of his rank, given a pretty excruciating appraisal, then shipped out in disgrace without any credit for his five victories. It took him a year to gain proper recognition. God help the flyer, however brilliant, who finds himself on the wrong side of political expediency.

As Overton pithily remarked 'I know that shit flows downhill but it seemed to me that this was a long way down.' Quite: the officer who'd binned him had led sorties over the line and had cynically and reprehensibly sacrificed a talented subordinate. He was the only pilot to be trashed though others might have been in the firing line. The high command faced a near-mutiny over such shabby and hypocritical treatment. Oddly enough some aces, such as Cecil Foster, with nine victories, never did cross the forbidden line. Overton wrote the foreword to Cecil Foster's memoirs and comments on this having been the exception rather than the norm.

Overton's unsavoury fate didn't deter others. That April, Hal Fischer, who had already scored twice, gave chase to a quartet of MiGs, as they fled across the river. His wingman was running on fumes so Fischer sent him back. Three more MiGs appeared but even at 7 to 1, Fischer wasn't blinking. This was real MiG madness and they were all well-trained Russian pilots. Fischer was on the tail of one, but two more were on his. At 400 metres the Soviet flyer opened fire and Fischer's luck ran out. He survived but was captured and spent over two years as a guest of the Chinese. That kind of dire experience was probably the perfect cure for MiG madness.

Clear skies over Zion

The conflict between the emerging state of Israel and her Arab neighbours began after a savage, messy six-month struggle following the expiry of the British Mandate in Palestine. With the declaration of independence, the war became more widespread, often characterised by atrocities on both sides. The struggle continued with further wars in 1956, 1976, 1973 and in the 1980s. Air power was to be crucial and the Israeli Air Force (IAF) swiftly established itself as an elite combat force with a number of pilots who would soon qualify as aces.

At first it was pretty desperate. Arms embargoes meant it was impossible for the fledgling Israeli state to acquire fighters. American pilot Lou Lenart, a veteran of the war against Japan, was determined to help recruit foreign Jewish flyers to form an ad hoc air force. Bizarrely, one of the few nations ready to sell weapons was Czechoslovakia, its puppet Soviet regime desperate for foreign currency. In a telling irony, the aircraft offered for sale were Me 109s, or a rather a Heath Robinson local variant with cobbled together parts. These weren't overly impressive, as Lenart commented:

> This plane was the worst piece of crap I have ever flown. It was not even an airplane. It was put together by the Czechs from mismatched parts left behind by the Nazis. The airframe was that of an Me 109 but the propeller and engine came out of a Heinkel bomber. You can't make a plane that way. But it was all we could get, so we took it.

On his first flight he nearly ditched in the sea. He described the plane as a Lamborghini with an old tractor engine, worse, the terrible synchronisation could result in his shooting his propeller off – 1914 style. Still, there was no time to lose:

> Every night we got bulletins from Israel. The Arab Legion with tanks and artillery was attacking near Jerusalem. Syrian forces had crossed the Jordan [River]. The Egyptian Army, with Spitfires, tanks, and artillery, was advancing up the coast road toward Tel Aviv. There's a kibbutz [communal settlement] on the frontier called Yad Mordechai. Three Egyptian battalions were attacking a force of 140. Even the kibbutz women fought in the trenches, firing World War I Enfields. They held out for five days before the Egyptians stormed the place and captured it.

Only six of these monstrous hybrids could be sourced and two were lost in transit. By now the Arab offensive had gained real momentum, advancing to a mere 17 miles from Tel Aviv. On 29 May 1948, Lenart with Modi Alon, Ezer Weizman and Eddie Cohen took to the air in an attempt to stem this inexorable advance, temporarily halted by a successful partial bridge demolition. This was true David and Goliath stuff. It was do or die; to prevent the Arabs from repairing the bridge and rolling unstoppably on. The odds were unfortunate. Some 6,000 troops, well-armed and well-equipped with AA guns, awaited them. Of the four pilots, only Lenart had ever flown a combat mission:

> We attack. The guns malfunction; the bomb releases balk. I look right and left and see nobody. Anti aircraft fire is ferocious. Six thousand Egyptians are putting up everything they've got. Eddie Cohen, a wonderful, brave pilot from South Africa, must have run into too much of it. His plane doesn't come back. I manage to put one 70-kilogram bomb onto a concentration of trucks and troops in the town square of Ishdud. Modi and Ezer do what they can. It's a mess. We straggle back, having inflicted minimal damage. But the shock to the Egyptians is overwhelming. To be attacked from the air by four Messerschmitt 109s with the Star of David on the side!

If their daring mission had not caused the enemy much serious harm, the shock to morale proved decisive, allowing Israeli ground forces to recover the initiative:

> The Egyptians are thrown into disorder. Israeli intelligence intercepts this dispatch from the brigade commander to Cairo: 'We were heavily attacked by enemy aircraft and we are scattering'. The Egyptian Army deflected to the east, to link with other Arab forces besieging Jerusalem. Tel Aviv was saved, and so was the nation. Sometime later I got a chance to speak with several Egyptian officers who were there that day. They said that the soldiers in the column were certain that these four planes, our piece-of-crap Messerschmitts, were just the tip of the spear, that the Jews had hundreds more, poised to attack and destroy them all.

Lenart's raid proved a game changer.

In 1956 Israel, allied with France and Britain, mounted an attack on Egypt across the wastes of Sinai. President Nasser had fortified his frontier with a series of strong firebases though these were fatally spread without mutual support capacity. Militarily the war was a success but pressure from both America and

The **Dassault M.D. 450 Ouragan ('Hurricane')** was a French fighter-bomber, the first jet-powered plane to enter French service in 1952. It served in diminishing roles into the 1980s but was adopted quite early by the Israelis who also swiftly acquired its successor, the **Dassault M.D. 452 Mystère**. This first went into French service in 1954 and was armed with twin 30 mm DEFA cannon. It became largely obsolescent quite quickly as the pace of design heated up. Still, it proved a match for the MiG-15.

A Dassault Mystère IVA.

Russia cancelled out the Allies' gains. On paper Nasser had 60 per cent greater strength in the air than Israel, mainly MiG-15s, and Vampire jets. Israel could field Mystère IVs, Ouragans and Vautours. In the first two days of fighting there were 164 dogfights which saw the Egyptians lose five MiGs and four Vampires. Israeli losses, which included two Mystères, were brought down by intense ground fire.

Operation *Focus*

In the spring of 1967 Israel faced a formidable coalition of encircling enemies: Egypt, Jordan and Syria, with support from Iraq, Saudi Arabia, Kuwait, Algeria and others. It was their combined intention to entirely crush the Jewish state. Israelis were fighting for their very survival. In the air the Arabs outnumbered them by at least 3 to 1. Both the Egyptians and Syrians had been equipped by the Soviets and had several

Israeli McDonnell Douglas F-4E Phantom II at Tel Nof, Israel, 2007.

squadrons of the latest MiG-21s, MiG-19s and Sukhoi fighters. Israel was apparently outgunned; she could field 70 Mirage IIICJs, deployed in three squadrons and six back-up formations of aged Ouragans, Mystères and Super-Mystères.

The build-up to the Six-Day War was the 'War for Water'. Tensions below the Golan Heights were already rising in April when Israeli *kibbutzim* attempted peaceful ploughing of a disputed strip south of the Sea of Galilee. This produced a sharp response from Syrian artillery, triggering an even sharper response from IAF fighter-bombers. The Syrian Air Force upped the stakes by scrambling some of its MiG-21s – state-of-the-art kit.

Israeli Mirages from 101 Squadron were sent up in the early afternoon. Captains Iftah Spector and Benyamin Romah engaged a pair of MiGs. Like rutting stags the four warplanes converged, then sheared off to manoeuvre. It was an old-fashioned twist and turn dogfight, the Mirages trying to get behind their fleet opponents. Spector managed it – first he got above, then slipped expertly onto his target's tail and brought him down with a surgical burst. The surviving MiG made a run for it, hotly pursued by Romah who couldn't get a clear shot in. By now the dogfight had moved from the skies above the Syrian town of Kuneitra clear to the rooftops of Damascus. The Israeli was on a parallel course to the Syrian, braking towards the MiG at full throttle and, with his afterburner, managed to get slotted in behind. Time was running out – he only managed on speculative burst. Good shooting as it turned out; he brought the Syrian down in flames.

As Arab forces massed on Israel's borders on 5 June confident of their superiority but, at the core, disunited and desperately unready, Major General Mordechai Hod, commanding the IAF was very ready. Quietly, Israel had begun mustering her citizen army. As the foundation block of her planned campaign, she intended to reduce the odds in the air by eliminating them on the ground. At 07.45 that Monday they struck. For three hours the Egyptian Air Force was to be the unhappy target of Operation *Focus*. In those three hours the Six Day War was decided, together with the future of the Middle East.

Israeli flyers came in low, under the radar screen. The moment to strike wasn't chosen at random. The IAF had calculated

The **Dassault Mirage III** was a single-seat jet fighter which came into French service in 1961. The Israelis bought mainly the IICJ. After the Six Day War France imposed an embargo on further sales so Israel started her own programme. The result was the Israeli Aircraft Industries IAI Nesher. Sixty-one were built and would see service in the Yom Kippur War. They were refurbished and sold to Argentina in the 1970s.

(correctly) that the bulk of enemy personnel would be travelling from home to base after an early breakfast, totally unsuspecting. The first wave struck 19 Egyptian airfields in Sinai, the Nile Valley, the Delta and around Cairo. Around 500 sorties were flown and 309 out of 340 warplanes were destroyed on the ground. All of their Soviet Tu-16 bombers, Ilyushin II-28s and Sukhoi Su-7s were blitzed; totalled together with the bulk of their top-end MiGs.

Egypt's allies, Jordan, Syria and Iraq, believing the cock and bull emanating from Egyptian radio, assumed all was going swimmingly. They commenced bombing and strafing sorties. It was a mistake. With Egyptian strength fully vanquished, the IAF turned its full attention towards her allies. By evening on 5 June, Jordan had no air force left, Syria and Iraq had been severely emasculated. By the end of the second day, 416 Arab planes had been disposed of, mostly on the ground without ever firing a single round. Dogfights had been few and furious. IAF had downed 58 for an overall loss of 26 of their own.

Operation *Rimon 20*

Despite the resounding humiliation of the Six Day War, Egypt was soon thirsting for la Revanche. For the next three years both sides fought a desultory 'War of Attrition'. Israel maintained virtual hegemony in the skies for most of this. Nasser turned to Russia who obliged and massively beefed up Egyptian air-defence capability. This, though vehemently denied by the Egyptians, presented Israel with a dilemma. While she was not prepared to cede control of the skies, she did not want to take on the Soviets directly for fear of escalation. The Russians were less fastidious and attacked Tel Aviv's planes both from the ground and in the air. The IAF decided to confront this emerging threat head on.

This would be in the form of an ambush. Operation *Rimon* ('Pomegranate') *20* (a variation on an earlier plan), would begin when the bait, an attack by Israeli F-4E Phantoms on an Egyptian radar base south and east of Suez and an outwardly routine patrol by Mirages over Egyptian airspace in the far south, would be dangled. Once vengeful MiGs took to the skies these would be drawn westwards into the teeth of Israeli reinforcements swooping in from the east.

At 14.00 on 30 July 1970 the first Israeli planes attacked ground radar. Flying to the east the four Mirages, looking like mere observers, all had teeth. In addition to their usual armament each carried a brace of A1M-9D Sidewinder missiles. The Soviets swallowed the bait, so up soared the MiGs, lots of them. As the would-be hunters closed to 20 km, the wolves in sheep's clothing turned to bare their very sharp fangs. The Mirages did not manoeuvre entirely according to plan. Instead of drawing the enemy west, they ended up charging head on. From the opposite direction the Phantoms were sweeping in, intending to attack the MiGs from behind and below in classic style as they attempted to give chase to the Mirages. It is often said that no plan ever survives first contact with the enemy and this melée was a classic example. The ambush swiftly spiralled into a messy dogfight.

Avraham Salmon spotted one MiG chasing a pair of Phantoms. His well-aimed A1M-9D obliterated the Russian. Another Israeli, Asher Snir, in the swirling heart of the brawl, latched

---

The **McDonnell Douglas F-4 Phantom** was a large, versatile tandem two-seater fighter bomber. Introduced in late 1960, it proved an excellent weapons platform, though not initially armed with guns. Later variants incorporated an M61 Vulcan Rotary cannon.

onto another MiG and unleashed one of his Sidewinders. It smacked into the Russian's underbelly. The pilot managed to eject but didn't survive the drop:

> One of Mirages (flown by Asher Snir) fired an air-to-air missile seconds after the battle began. The missile hit a MiG and set it on fire. The pilot bailed out; the aircraft went into a spin and dropped like a stone from 30,000 ft. The Russian pilot's parachute opened right away – it's not supposed to: chutes are designed to open automatically at 10,000 ft., so their wearers don't freeze or suffocate at high altitudes.

Snir didn't have it all his own way; being without a wingman, he failed to spot another MiG coming up behind. A Soviet missile crashed into his engine exhaust, wrecking the tail-plane. Despite the damage he managed to nurse the crippled Mirage clear of the fight and a safe emergency landing on friendly tarmac. The vortex of high-speed battle dragged in fresh blood. The Israelis were both more skilled and aggressive but heavily outnumbered. Reinforcements were sent up. Another quartet of Mirages which had been lurking just outside radar range weighed in. One developed mechanical problems and, escorted by his wingman, beat a retreat. Captain Spector – who we last encountered over Damascus and who now had eight kills under his belt – and another Mirage, piloted by Michael Tzuk, took their places. Tzuk also encountered difficulties and had to turn back. Spector ploughed on alone.

The Israeli Phantoms hunting in pairs took fewer risks but weren't knocking down any MiGs. Aviem Sella split from his wingman and stalked a lone MiG but couldn't get a lock. The Russian executed a tight turn and came head on. Immelmann would have been proud of Sella's own counter-move which put him above and behind:

> By this time I'd realized the Russian pilot was inexperienced; he didn't know how to handle his aircraft in a combat situation. At

15,000ft he proved this fact by trying to escape in a steep dive to 700ft. All we had to do was follow him and lock our radar onto him – and fire a missile. There was a tremendous explosion – but the MiG came out of the cloud of smoke apparently unharmed. That made me mad and I fired a second missile – which turned out to be unnecessary. The Russian aircraft had, in fact, been severely damaged by the first missile; suddenly, it burst into flames and fell apart. By the time the second missile reached it, it wasn't there anymore. Despite this biblical end, the pilot managed to eject safely.

By now, the fight had raged for two whole minutes. Both sides were running low on fuel and the Russians were in an understandable hurry to depart. The IAF didn't give up. Avihu Bin-Nun saw a MiG, flying at less than 2,000 feet, hotly pursued by two Israelis. One shot a missile but the range was too great. The other had none left to fire and was closing in to use his cannon when Bin-Nun's A1M-7 missile destroyed the MIG and its unlucky pilot. A bit of inter-unit rivalry was involved here:

> Suddenly we found ourselves, me and my number 2, along with a lone 117 Squadron jet, pursuing a MiG flying at low level and almost at the speed of sound. As we saw it, the biggest threat was that the 117 pilot would claim our MiG. We launched a 'Sparrow', though one shouldn't at that altitude and in those conditions, just so that 117 wouldn't get him!

Avraham Salmon was chasing another Russian. The MiG jinked to avoid his remaining missile. Soon the formidable Spector was in on the hunt. He fired two rockets, at least one of which hit, but the plane flew on seemingly unscathed. Salmon kept up the pursuit, getting close enough to expend his remaining cannon shells. He assumed the Russian got away but, years later, he found out the plane had gone down, killing the pilot. The fight had lasted three minutes and five MiGs had bought it. That was 5-0 to the IAF who'd rather made their point. Admittedly every IAF pilot in the sky that day was an ace. Later that year

Golda Meir could confidently assert: 'How do I know there are Russian pilots in Egypt; very simply because we had shot down four Soviet planes that were flown by Soviet pilots.'

South Atlantic – Blackbirds and Falcons

Well I think that some of the experts rather exaggerate the value, the strength of the Argentinean air force … their Mirage aircraft really are a decade behind the Harrier, and beyond that their other aircraft are not particularly modern, some of them are very old and the Harrier is a very effective aircraft. So I think we must not exaggerate their air situation…

The words of UK Defence Secretary John Nott in May 1982 reek of the armchair strategist's complacency. British sailors on HMS *Sheffield* – those who survived – might well have expressed a different view. Underestimating the enemy's capacity and

Sea Harriers FA2 in the Persian Gulf, 1998.

resolve are fundamental errors and would reap a bitter harvest in the South Atlantic.

The Fuerza Aerea Argentina (Argentinian Air Force) had both numbers and available land bases on their side, though the flying distance from airfields meant they had very little time over the actual combat zone. The Argentinean pilots were brave and well-trained, by both the French and Israelis. Ironically, it was the head of the junta's air force that was least bullish about the invasion. His worries were sound: from some sorties as many as 75 per cent of pilots would fail to return.

Fighting over water is different to battling over dry land and none of their pilots had any combat experience. The Royal Navy could deploy a formidable arsenal of missiles and guns and John Nott was correct in boasting that British pilots and planes were much better. An American expert, Colonel James MacManaway, quipped it was like pitting blackbirds against falcons. Argentina would have to rely on ageing Skyhawk A4Ps, the Mirage IIIAs and Vs ('Daggers' – the Israeli Nesher refurbished). Britain had the Sea Harrier. The Mirages were far faster but lacked the Harrier's formidable agility.

In air-to-air combat the Mirages could find themselves being 'viffed' (vectoring in forward flight). For the Argentine pilots this was both disconcerting and potentially fatal. As they approached from behind to commence an attack run, the Harrier pilot

The **British Aerospace Sea Harrier** – Short Take-Off and Vertical Landing/Vertical Take-Off and Landing (V/STOL) jet fighter came into service in April 1980 as Sea Harrier FRS1 – soon dubbed the 'Shar'. Its primary role was to provide air defence for carriers. The plane was very successful and served until 2006 with the Royal Navy.

would apply downward thrust which causes his aircraft to shoot upwards ('viff') and slow dramatically. A Mirage cannot hope to reduce speed so swiftly and so overshoots his intended target. A Sidewinder missile from the Harrier closes the kill. Though this was a brilliant tactic, none of the Harriers' victories seem to have actually been scored this way!

The Harriers deployed to the South Atlantic in April 1982 would be protecting the Task Force's two vulnerable carriers, HMS *Invincible* and HMS *Hermes*. There were 20 of the 'jump jets' on board these. Despite the ministers' bland assurances, there could be no question that enemy Mirages were both swifter and far more numerous. Furthermore, they'd be fighting over their own home waters or what they believed to be theirs. The Shar was as yet unproven in combat but its baptism took place on the morning of 1 May.

A brace of Harriers on patrol over Port Stanley picked up on three slow-moving aircraft coming up from the airfield. These were in fact lumbering Beechcraft T-34 trainers. Wisely, on realising they were being stalked, these sought refuge in low cloud. One Harrier loosed off a few 30-mm cannon rounds but the quarry escaped. That afternoon it was the Mirages' turn. A three-strong flight was picked up by HMS *Glamorgan* and two jump jets scrambled. The Mirages appeared to flee but soon swept back round again for a second attempt; distance was 25 miles and closing.

The Brits charged head on ready for 'hooking' – the lead plane barrels in head first while his wingman splits to try and get behind. The idea is the enemy will be so distracted by the bull rushing in they won't spot the matador. Nor did they; the wingman's Sidewinder blasted one of the Mirages. This was the first of a score of kills. No Harriers were lost in air-to-air combat, though ground fire downed two. This duel was reminiscent of many of those of earlier wars but the world was changing, the shift in competing technologies moving way faster than the sound barrier.

THE LAST ACES?

On a dusty tarmac, about 20 miles from downtown Phoenix, Capt. Joseph Stenger stands in 109-degree heat, barely sweating. A 32-year-old fighter pilot with the slicked-back hair, steady eyes, and ropey forearms you see on movie posters, he is admiring an equally impressive piece of flying machinery: the F-35 Lightning II fighter. In his green flight suit, and standing a little over 6 feet tall, Stenger is nearly face to snout with this menacing jet. It's his job to figure out what it can do in combat, and to teach that to hundreds of other fighter pilots.

THE AIR ACE WAS A CHILD of industrial war. Even now it is barely a century since man first achieved powered flight which a hundred years earlier had seemed merely a dream. Within the 20th century, aside from the innovations spurred by two world wars, the most destructive in history, those first few yards of flying led to the B-29, which could deliver the weapon of Armageddon halfway round the world, to supersonic travel, and ultimately those few giant steps on the moon. The knights of the air in these pages were very much part of that, yet they still carry resonances of earlier, timeless conflict and the nobility of the knightly warrior. Manfred von Richthofen was the Achilles of the Great War, a hero and a killer.

The battle for supremacy in the skies has not just been about the steel and sinew of the pilot but about competing technologies. All heroism aside, generally the man with the better aircraft will win; it is as simple as that. By its very nature industrial war is dominated by technological development. Achilles would not have seen too many differences between his fight with Hector on the dusty Plain of Troy in 1250 BC and the famous duel between Jarnac and La Châtaigneraie over two and a half thousand years later in 1547. Steel instead of bronze of course but still with swords. None of the Great War aces would have quite understood the Soviet/IAF clashes over Sinai, less than half a century after the trenches. Enter the fighter of the future, as described in *Popular Science*:

> The F-35 is the most sophisticated fighter ever built. It is stealthy, so it can appear the size of a golf ball to enemy radar, if it's detected at all. It can also jam enemy radar – or make it seem there are 100 golf-ball-size targets in the sky. It can travel at Mach 1.6. It carries a 25 mm cannon, air-to-air missiles, two 2,000-pound guided bombs, and four external laser-guided bombs. But what truly sets it apart is its brain, 8 million lines of software code – more than any fighter in history – fusing navigation, communication, and targeting systems. That's a very long way from an SE5A and almost exactly one hundred years on.
>
> Most in the military see the plane as the key to America's continued air superiority, and yet it could also spell the beginning of the end for an iconic American profession. The F-35 is so high-tech, so automated, so smart, connected, that in May, the secretary of the Navy, Ray Mabus, declared: The F-35 'should be, and almost certainly will be, the last manned strike fighter aircraft the Department of the Navy will ever buy or fly. If another manned fighter comes up, great. If not, that sinks it for the next generation.'

It is very likely that the technology of aerial warfare will advance so far that it can dispense with the hitherto fundamental, if squishy and organic bit – the pilot. Many missions are now carried out by pilotless drones, controlled remotely over vast distances. The desk jockey in charge doesn't need to be a Brylcreem boy full of aggressive, focused youth and testosterone. He can be an overweight geek with acne and issues and still get the job done. He'll never be a hero but he might, if obesity doesn't get him, make it to pensionable age.

It is entirely possible that the fighter ace, so long the pin-up of modern war, becomes a total anachronism. That won't diminish his popularity, probably quite the opposite. He joins the nostalgia movement. We love to glamorize that past. It never really was glamorous, certainly not in the air but the comfort of 'our finest hour' offers sanctuary from the sordid and insoluble horrors of the 21st century. And perhaps above all nostalgias, 1940 and the Battle of Britain has become the most potent and enduring. The 'few' have become the ultimate symbolism of courage, sacrifice and nobility and deservedly so for they were all of those and more. Theirs is the shining example and as long as we remember, all the aces may be assured of their rightful place in history.

SOURCES

A book of this type relies mainly upon secondary sources and most of those which have been consulted are referred to below. Individuals who have greatly assisted us include Trevor Sheehan of Defence Photography and Codi von Richthofen.

INTRODUCTION & CHAPTER 1

Permission to reproduce the *War in the Air* and *Skygod* (http://historynet/ mig-madness-the-air-war-over-korea.htm (retrieved 4 November 2016), has been kindly given by the Poetry Foundation and by Alexander Nemerov. This applies also to *Skygod* by Grover C. Norwood and the verses by Robert Crawford. Extracts from *The Flying Machine and Modern Literature* by Laurence Goldstein are reproduced by kind permission of Indiana University Press though the quote starting 'The Heavens are their Battlefields…' is actually attributed to David Lloyd George, and is footnoted as appearing in *The Great Crusade: Extracts from Speeches Delivered During the War* (New York, George H. Doran, 1918), p. 89. The passage from 633 Squadron appears by kind permission of Orion Books Limited and those from The Last Enemy by kind permission of Vintage/Penguin Books Limited. The quote about von Richthofen is from P. Kilduff, *Richthofen – Beyond the Legend of the Red Baron* (London, Cassell, 1993), p. 7.

CHAPTER 2

The opening verse by Cecil Lewis is quoted in Alan Clark, *Aces High* (London, Cassell, 2012 edition), p. 185. Much of the technical detail in this and subsequent chapters is from Clark's excellent book and also from the less well known Joseph A. Phelan, *Heroes & Aeroplanes of the Great War 1914–1918* (London, Arthur Barker, 1967), a real anorak's treasury filled with technical detail and superbly illustrated. The quotation from Sopwith features on p. 11. *The RFC Mess Song* sung to the tune of *Tonight's the Night* and that to the tune of *We've Come up from Somerset* all feature in *Aces High*. Lieutenant Reid's adventure is drawn from http://spartacus-educational/com/fwwdogfights.htm (retrieved 21 November 2016). Second Lieutenant Bott's experiences are taken from M. Richardson, *Eyewitness to the Somme* (Barnsley, Pen & Sword, 2016) pp. 161–163. The experiences of Lieutenant Tudor-Hart are related in Peter Hart, *The Somme* (London, Weidenfeld & Nicolson, 2005), p. 201.

CHAPTER 3

The header quote by von Richthofen features in Alan Clark, *Aces High*. For much of the general narrative and detail in this chapter we've relied on Peter Hart, *Aces Falling* (London, Weidenfeld & Nicolson, 2007). The von Richthofen quote is from http://www.eyewitnesstohistory.com/richthofen.htm (retrieved 25 November 2016). The quotes about Mick Mannock and from Eddie Rickenbacker are featured on http://spartacus-educational.com/FWWdogfights.htm (retrieved 25 November 2016). George Guynemer's narrative is from http://en.wikipedia.org/wiki/georgesguynemer (retrieved 25 November 2016). The Kiffin Yates Rockwell quote is from Clark, *Aces High*. The account of Barker's amazing fight is also related in Clark, *Aces High*.

CHAPTER 4

For the overall history of World War II in the air, we're indebted to Walter J. Boyne, *Clash of Wings* (New York, Touchstone 1997). General information on the Battle of Britain comes from Len Deighton's classic *Fighter: the true story of the Battle of Britain* (London, Jonathan Cape, 1977) and Richard Hough and Denis Richards, *Battle of Britain – the Jubilee History* (London, Hodder & Stoughton, 1989). *Easter 1916* is by W. B. Yeats. Pilot Officer Beard's experiences may be found at eyewitnesshistory.com/airbattle.htm (retrieved 12 December 2016). Flight Lieutenant Robinson's account is from bbc.co.uk/history/ww2peopleswar/stories/53 (retrieved 12 December 2016) and Squadron Leader Pinfold's story is at no 93 in the same series (retrieved 12 December).

For the Desert War generally, we have used John Sadler, El Alamein 1942 (Stroud, Amberley 2010) and the account of Clive Caldwell's experiences is to be found at ww2/today.com/29th-august-19141-dogfight-over-the-desert (retrieved 12 December 2016). For the Siege of Malta and the career of Adrian Warburton, we've used James Holland, Fortress Malta (London, Phoenix, 2003).

CHAPTER 5

Once again, we've relied quite heavily on Boyne's *Clash of Wings*. For the Eastern Front we've used many of the excellent single-volume accounts, particularly those of Alan Clark and Richard Overy. Inna Pasportnikova is cited in Reina Pennington, *Wings, Women, and War: Soviet Airwomen in World War II Combat* (University Press of Kansas, 2001). Ivan Borisenko is cited in Bruce Myles, *Night Witches: the untold story of Soviet women in combat* (Mainstream, 1981). For D-Day and the battle for North-West Europe we've also relied on a significant number of secondary sources and Chuck Yeager's experiences can be found at eyewitnesstohistory.om/shot.htm, retrieved 22 December 2016.

CHAPTER 6

In writing about Korea we've used Max Hastings' first-class single-volume account, *The Korean War* (2010 Pan edition). More eyewitness testimony is taken from http://www.historynet.com/mig-madness-the-air-war-over-korea. htm (retrieved 6 December 2016). For Arab-Israeli combats, we've relied on Chaim Herzog's superb history, *The Arab-Israeli Wars* (Cassell, 1982), still the best overall account. Additional detail on Arab/Israeli dogfights comes from: businessinsider.com/four-israeli-aircraft-stopped-a-huge-arab-army-in-1948.2014-5?R=T and also from: sixdaywar.co.uk/independent-dogfight-ofapril-7th.htm – both retrieved on 6 December 2016. General background information on the Falklands War comes from The *Sunday Times*' history of the conflict (London, Sphere Books, 1982) while detail of the Harrier vs Mirage clashes is gleaned from: https://theaviationist.com/2012/05/22/sea-harrier-the-forgotten-hero-that-won-the-war-in-the-falklands-to-be-replaced-by-the-f-35b/ (retrieved on 7 December 2016). *Who's for the Game* is by Jessie Pope.

POSTSCRIPT

Information on the F-35 comes from an article originally published in the January/February 2016 issue of *Popular Science* – http://www.popsci.com/last-fighter-pilot – retrieved 8 December 2016.